Birds of Florida

Todd Telander

FALCONGUIDES

GUILFORD, CONNECTICUT
HELENA, MONTANA

AN IMPRINT OF GLOBE PEQUOT PRESS

To my wife, Kirsten, my children, Miles and Oliver, and my parents, all of whom have supported and encouraged me through the years. Special thanks to Mike Denny for his expert critique of the illustrations.

To buy books in quantity for corporate use or incentives, call **(800) 962-0973** or e-mail **premiums@GlobePequot.com**.

FSC
www.fsc.org

MIX
Paper from
responsible sources
FSC® C005010

FALCONGUIDES®

Copyright © 2012 Morris Book Publishing, LLC
Illustrations © 2012 Todd Telander

FalconGuides is an imprint of Globe Pequot Press.
Falcon Field Guide is a trademark and Falcon, FalconGuides, and Outfit Your Mind are registered trademarks of Morris Book Publishing, LLC.

Illustrations: Todd Telander
Text design: Sheryl P. Kober
Project editor: Julie Marsh
Layout: Sue Murray

Library of Congress Cataloging-in-Publication Data is available on file.
ISBN 978-0-7627-7419-7
Printed in the United States of America

10 9 8 7 6 5 4 3 2 1

Contents

Nonpasserines

Passerines

Introduction

With its southern tip jutting into the tropical Gulf of Mexico and its northern end part of mainland North America, Florida is home to, or is visited by, an incredible variety and number of bird species. From dry scrubland and pine forests to lush mangroves and coastal shores, the state supports birdlife for resident breeders, seasonal visitors, as well as those passing through on migration to and from South America and Canada. This guide is a distillation of the most common birds seen here, but also includes a few rarities that can only be found in Florida within the United States.

Notes about the Species Accounts

Order

The order of species listed in this guide is based on the latest version of the *Check-List of North American Birds,* published by the American Ornithologist's Union. The arrangement of some groups, especially within the nonpasserines, may be slightly different than that of older field guides, but, in an effort to remain current, I have used the most recent arrangement here.

Names

For each entry, I have included the common name as well as the scientific name. Since common names tend to vary regionally, or there may be more than one common name for each species, the universally accepted scientific name of genus and species (such as *Mycteria americana,* for the Wood Stork) is more reliable to be certain of identification. Also, one can often learn interesting facts about a bird by the English translation of its Latin name.

Families

Birds are grouped into families based on similar traits and genetics. It can often be helpful when trying to identify an unfamiliar bird to first place it into a family, which will reduce your search to a smaller group. For example, if you see a long-legged, long-billed bird lurking slowly in the shallows, you can begin your search in the family group of Ardeidae, or Herons and Egrets.

Size

The size given for each bird is the average length, from the tip of the bill to the end of the tail if the bird was laid out flat. Sometimes females and males vary in size, and this is mentioned in the text. Size can be misleading if you are looking at a small bird that happens to have a very long tail or bill. More effective is the use of relative size, or judging the size difference between two or more species.

Season

The season given in the accounts is when most individuals occur in Florida. Some species are year-round residents that breed here. Others may spend only summers or winters here, and some may be transient, only stopping during the spring or fall during migration. Even if only part of the year is indicated for a species, be aware that there may be individuals that arrive earlier or remain for longer than that time frame. Plumage also changes with the season for many birds, and this is indicated in the text and illustrations.

Habitat

A bird's habitat is one of the first clues to its identification. Note the environment where you see a bird and compare it with the description listed. For example, Cattle Egrets and Snowy Egrets are similar, but Cattle Egrets are found in drier fields and pastures while Snowy Egrets prefer swamps and open water.

Illustrations

I have illustrated the adult bird in the plumage most likely to be encountered during the season(s) it is in Florida. If it is likely that you will find more than one plumage during this time, I have illustrated the alternate plumage as well. For birds that are sexually dimorphic (females and males look different), I have included illustrations of both sexes. Other plumages such as juveniles and alternate morphs are described in the text.

Bird Topography and Terms

Bird topography is the outer surface of the bird and how the parts fit together. Below is a diagram outlining the most commonly used terms we use when describing the feathers and bare parts of a bird.

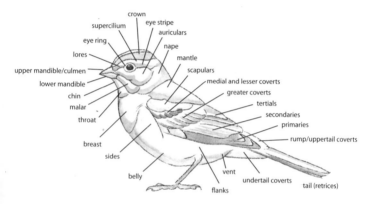

NONPASSERINES

Canada Goose,
Branta canadensis
Family Anatidae (Ducks, Geese)
Size: Large, but highly variable
Season: Winter in Florida
Habitat: Marshes, grasslands, public parks, golf courses

The Canada Goose is our most common goose and is often found in suburban settings. It is vegetarian, foraging on land for grass, seeds, and grain, or in the water by upending like the dabbling ducks. It has a heavy body with short, thick legs and a long neck. It is overall barred gray-brown with a white rear, short black tail, black neck, and a white patch running under the neck to behind the eye. During its powerful flight in classic "V" formation, the white across the rump makes a semicircular patch between the tail and back. Its voice is a loud *honk*. The illustration shows an adult.

Wood Duck, *Aix sponsa*
Family Anatidae (Ducks, Geese)
Size: 18"
Season: Year-round in Florida
Habitat: Wooded ponds and swamps

The regal Wood Duck is among the dabbling ducks, or those that tip headfirst into shallow water to pluck aquatic plants and animals from the bottom. The male is long-tailed, small-billed, with a dark back, light buffy flanks, and sharp black-and-white head patterning. It also sports a bushy head crest that droops behind the nape. The female is gray-brown with spotting along the undersides and a conspicuous white, teardrop-shaped eye patch. Both sexes swim with their heads angled downwards as if in a nod, and they have sharp claws to cling to branches and snags. The illustration shows a breeding male, below, and a female, above.

Mallard, *Anas platyrhynchos*
Family Anatidae (Ducks, Geese)
Size: 23"
Season: Year-round resident
Habitat: Virtually any water environment, parks, urban areas

The ubiquitous Mallard is the most abundant duck in the northern hemisphere. It is a classic dabbling duck, plunging its head into the water with its tail up, searching for aquatic plants, animals, and snails, although it will also eat worms, seeds, insects, and even mice. Noisy and quacking, it is a heavy but strong flier. The male has a dark head with green or blue iridescence, a white neck ring, and a large yellow bill. The underparts are pale with a chestnut-brown breast. The female is plain brownish with buffy, scalloped markings. It also has a dark eye line and orangey bill with a dark center. The speculum is blue on both sexes, and the tail coverts often curl upward. Mallards form huge floating flocks called "rafts." To achieve flight, a Mallard lifts straight into the air without running. The illustration shows a breeding male, below, and a female, above.

Mottled Duck, *Anas fulvigula*
Family Anatidae (Ducks, Geese)
Size: 22"
Season: Year-round in Florida
Habitat: Most aquatic areas, coastal marshes

A very close relative of the Mallard, the Mottled Duck is a common dabbling duck with similar foraging habits and quacking voice. In appearance, both sexes are similar to the female Mallard only darker and slightly larger. It is buffy brown overall with a lighter head and neck, and with no white on the tail. The male has a bright yellow bill; that of the female is darker. The greenish speculum is seen primarily in flight. Some consider the Mottled Duck to be a subspecies of the Mallard. The illustration shows an adult male.

American Widgeon,
Anas americana
Family Anatidae (Ducks, Geese)
Size: 19"
Season: Winter in Florida
Habitat: Shallow ponds, fields

The American Widgeon is also known as the Baldpate, in reference to its white crown. A wary and easily alarmed duck, it feeds from the water's surface, often gleaning prey stirred up by the efforts of diving ducks. Its underside is a light cinnamon color with white undertail coverts, and its back is light brown. The male has a white crown and forehead with a very slight crest when seen in profile, and a glossy, dark green patch extending from the eye to back of the neck. A white wing covert patch can usually be seen on the folded wing but is more obvious in flight. The head of the female is unmarked and brownish. The illustration shows a breeding male, below, and a female, above.

Northern Shoveler,
Anas clypeata
Family Anatidae (Ducks, Geese)
Size: 19"
Season: Winter in Florida
Habitat: Shallow marshes, lakes, and bays

Also known as the Spoonbill Duck, the Northern Shoveler skims the surface of the water with neck extended to scoop up aquatic animals and plants with its long, spatula-like bill. It will also suck up the ooze from mud and strain it through bristles at the edge of its bill to retain worms, leeches, and snails. This medium-size duck seems top heavy due to its large bill. Plumage in the male is white beneath with a large, chestnut side patch and a dark green head and gray bill. The female is pale brownish overall with an orangey bill. The illustration shows a breeding male, below, and a female, above.

Blue-winged Teal, *Anas discors*
Family Anatidae (Ducks, Geese)
Size: 16"
Season: Winter in Florida
Habitat: Freshwater marshes and mud flats, wet agricultural areas

The Blue-winged Teal is a small duck that skims the water surface for aquatic plants and invertebrates, often forming large flocks. The male is mottled brown below with a prominent white patch near the hip area, dark above, and gray on the head with a white vertical crescent at the base of the bill. The female is brownish with scalloped flanks and a plain head with a dark eye line and pale at the lores. Both sexes have a light-blue wing patch visible in flight. Also known as the White-faced Teal. The illustration shows a breeding male, below, and a female, above.

Ring-necked Duck,
Aythya collaris
Family Anatidae (Ducks, Geese)
Size: 17"
Season: Winter in Florida
Habitat: Coastal marshes

The Ring-necked Duck is in the group of diving ducks that typically swim underwater to find plants and animal prey, although it may also behave like dabbling ducks and bob for food at the surface. This gregarious, small duck looks tall with a postlike head and neck and a peaked crown. The breeding male is stunning with its contrasting light-and-dark plumage and metallic, dark, brown-purple head. The base of the bill, which is gray with a white ring and black tip, is edged with white feathers. The female is more brownish overall with a white eye ring. The ring around the neck, for which it is named, is actually a very inconspicuous brownish band at the bottom of the neck in the male bird. Also known as the Ring-billed Duck. The illustration shows a breeding male, below, and a female, above.

Bufflehead, *Bucephala albeola*
Family Anatidae (Ducks, Geese)
Size: 14"
Season: Winter in Florida
Habitat: Inland lakes or sheltered coastal bays

The Bufflehead is a diminutive diving duck, indeed, the smallest duck in North America. Also known as the Bumblebee Duck, it forms small flocks as it forages the open water for aquatic plants and invertebrates. The puffy, rounded head seems large for the body and compared to the small, gray-blue bill. The breeding male is striking with a large white patch on the back half of its head, contrasting with the black front of its head and back. Its underside is white. The female is paler overall with an airfoil-shaped white patch behind the eye on a dark, gray-brown head. Flight is low to the water with rapid wing beats. The illustration shows a breeding male, below, and a female, above.

Red-breasted Merganser,
Mergus serrator
Family Anatidae (Ducks, Geese)
Size: 23"
Season: Winter in Florida
Habitat: Sheltered coastal waters

The mergansers are known as the Fishing Ducks or Saw-tooths. They dive and chase fish of considerable size underwater and secure their catch with their long, thin bill, which is serrated along the edges. Both male and female Red-breasted Mergansers sport a fine, long, two-parted crest. The male has a white band around the neck, a dark head, a red bill, and gray flanks. The female is grayish overall with a brown head. The nonbreeding male closely resembles the female. Flight is low and quick on pointed wings. The illustration shows a breeding male, below, and a female, above.

Pied-billed Grebe,
Podilymbus podiceps
Family Podicipedidae (Grebes)
Size: 13"
Season: Year-round resident in Florida
Habitat: Freshwater ponds and lakes

The Pied-billed Grebe is a secretive, small grebe that lurks in sheltered waters diving for small fish, leeches, snails, and crawfish. When alarmed or to avoid predatory snakes and hawks, it has the habit of sinking until only the head is above water until danger has passed. It is brownish overall, slightly darker above, with a tiny tail and short wings. The breeding adult has a conspicuous dark ring around the middle of the bill, missing in winter plumage. It nests on a floating mat of vegetation. The illustration shows a breeding adult.

American Flamingo,
Phoenicopterus ruber
Family Phoenicopteridae (Flamingos)
Size: 48"
Season: Winter in Florida
Habitat: Saltwater flats,
Florida Keys area

The rare American Flamingo walks slowly and steadily through shallows with its head upside down in the water, moving it from side to side to extract small aquatic prey and shrimp. It is unmistakable with its pink body, black wings, extremely long legs and neck, and thick, two-toned bill that bends down at its midpoint. It runs to take off and often flies in a flock forming long, single-file lines in the sky, emitting honking calls. Young Flamingos are very pale with gray on the back; they gradually acquire the pink plumage. The illustration shows an adult.

White-tailed Tropicbird,
Phaethon lepturus
Family Phaethontidae (Tropicbirds)
Size: 30"
Season: Spring, summer,
during migration
Habitat: Open coastal waters

The White-tailed Tropicbird is a graceful, tern-shaped bird often seen soaring to great heights. To feed, it drops and plunge-dives for fish and squid. Its plumage is white with contrasting black patches at the base of the primaries and long oblique black stripes along the inner wing. The head has a dark eye line and the bill is yellow-orange. The extremely long, delicate, inner tail feathers are conspicuous; they are lacking in the juvenile. Florida is the only reliable place to see this bird in the United States. The illustration shows an adult.

Wood Stork, *Mycteria americana*
Family Ciconiidae (Storks)
Size: 40"
Season: Year-round in Florida
Habitat: Salt or fresh open marshes

The Wood Stork is a large, somewhat unattractive bird with a white body, black flight feathers, and a featherless neck and head covered in blackish, scaly skin. The bill is long, decurved, and blunt at its tip. It forms flocks and feeds by probing its bill into the mud, stirring up prey such as fish and snakes. It flies with its neck outstretched in loose, unorganized groups. At rest it will stand motionless for an hour or more in a distinctive, upright posture with its bill tucked down and against the body. It roosts in mangrove or cypress trees and emits croaking sounds or chattering by snapping the upper and lower mandibles together. The illustration shows an adult.

Magnificent Frigatebird,
Fregata magnificens
Family Fregatidae (Frigatebirds)
Size: 40"
Season: Year-round in Florida
Habitat: Coastal, southern keys

The Magnificent Frigatebird can be seen soaring effortlessly for hours, high in the air off the coast. To feed, it skims the surface of the water in flight to snatch fish, or may steal food from other sea-birds. It has long, slender wings and a deeply forked tail. The bill is long and hooked. Males are black overall with a curious red throat patch that can be inflated like a balloon. Females have a white belly and sides. The illustration shows an adult female.

Northern Gannet,
Morus bassanus
Family Sulidae (Gannets)
Size: 36"
Season: Winter in Florida
Habitat: Open ocean close to shore

The name Gannet derives from "gander" and alludes to the goose-like shape of this seabird. Often forming very large groups, the Northern Gannet alternates rapid wing beats with soaring flight. To feed, it forms its body into a sleek arrow shape and dramatically plunges headfirst into the ocean, completely submerging itself to catch fish. Its body is sleek and white with black flight feathers. The upper part of the head is pale yellow; the bill is thick, pointed, and bluish. The eye seems small and is enveloped in a thin black ring and lores. The juvenile is dark and spotted with white. The illustration shows an adult.

Double-crested Cormorant,
Phalacrocorax auritus
Family Phalacrocoracidae (Cormorants)
Size: 32"
Season: Year-round resident in Florida
Habitat: Open fresh- or salt water

Named for the two long, white plumes that emerge from behind its eyes during breeding season, the Double-crested Cormorant is an expert swimmer that dives underwater to chase down fish. Because its plumage lacks the normal oils to repel water, it will stand with wings outstretched to dry itself. It is all black with a pale, glossy cast on the back and wings. The eye is bright green, the bill thin and hooked, and the throat patch and lores yellow. The illustration shows a breeding adult.

Anhinga, *Anhinga anhinga*
Family Anhingadae (Anhinga)
Size: 34"
Season: Year-round resident in Florida
Habitat: Freshwater ponds and swamps

With a cormorant-like body and snakelike neck, the Anhinga swims underwater to spear fish with its sharp, daggerlike bill. It can be seen with only its head above water or soaring high above the marshes and will often stand with wings outstretched to dry them. Its body is black with finely patterned white streaks; its tail is long, barred with white and tipped with brown. The female has a pale brown neck and head, while that of the male is all black. In breeding plumage, the male develops an upturned crest. The illustration shows an adult female.

American White Pelican,
Pelecanus erythrorhynchos
Family Pelecanidae (Pelicans)
Size: 62"
Season: Winter and spring in Florida
Habitat: Coastal waters,
open fresh water

One of our largest birds, the American White Pelican has a wing-span of over 9 feet and is white overall with black flight feathers. The massive bill is orange with a membranous, expandable throat pouch. In posture, it keeps its neck in a characteristic strong kink and holds its folded wings with a peak along the back. It often feeds in cooperative groups, swimming along, herding fish, and scooping them up by dipping the bill in the water. It never plunge-dives like the Brown Pelican. In breeding plumage, a strange horny growth appears on the upper mandible. The illustration shows a nonbreeding adult.

Brown Pelican,
Pelecanus occidentalis
Family Pelecanidae (Pelicans)
Size: 50"
Season: Year-round in Florida
Habitat: Coastal waters

The majestic Brown Pelican enlivens the coastal waters with its spectacular feeding process of plunge-diving for fish, headfirst, from some height. In flight it often cruises in formation inches from incoming swells, gaining lift and rarely needing to flap its wings. Its plumage is a bleached gray-brown overall with a white head and neck and a massive bill. In breeding, the head is pale yellow with a brown-red nape patch and a black strip down the back of the neck. Quite gregarious, it may nest in mangrove trees or in slight depressions in the sand or rocks. The illustration shows a breeding adult.

Least Bittern, *Ixobrychus exilis*
Family Ardeidae (Herons, Egrets)
Size: 13"
Season: Year-round in central and southern Florida; summer in northern Florida
Habitat: Fresh or brackish marshes

The Least Bittern is our smallest heron, secretive, and more often heard than seen. It creeps and clambers through densely vegetated marshes searching for frogs, invertebrates, and other aquatic creatures, emitting a soft cooing call or *kaw* when disturbed. It is rarely seen in flight. Its back is a dark blue-gray, its mid-wing and body a buffy brown with white streaking. The crown is dark gray and the bill is yellow and pointed. Legs and feet are yellow with long, thin toes for grasping clumps of vegetation. The female is paler along the back and crown. When alarmed, it will stand motionless with its head straight up, imitating a stalk of reeds. The illustration shows an adult male.

Great Blue Heron,
Ardea herodias
Family Ardeidae (Herons, Egrets)
Size: 46"
Season: Year-round in Florida
Habitat: Most aquatic areas, lakes, creeks, marshes

The Great Blue Heron is the largest heron in North America. Walking slowly through shallow water or fields, it stalks fish, crabs, and small vertebrates with the help of its massive bill. With long legs and neck, it is blue gray overall with a white face and heavy, yellow-orange bill. The crown is black and supports plumes of medium length. The front of the neck is white with distinct black chevrons fading into breast plumes. In flight, the neck is tucked back and wing beats are regular and labored. The illustration shows an adult.

Great Blue Heron (White Morph) or "Great White Heron"

Family Ardeidae (Herons, Egrets)
Size: 46"
Season: Year-round in Florida
Habitat: Most aquatic areas, lakes, creeks, marshes

Once considered to be a separate species, this is the white version of the Great Blue Heron at lower left. It is identical to the normal morph except in plumage color. Compare it with the Great Egret, which is smaller, has a thinner bill, and black legs. A hybrid between the Great Blue and the Great White exists, called the Wurdemann's Heron, which has a gray body and white head and neck. The illustration shows an adult.

Great Egret,
Ardea alba
Family Ardeidae (Herons, Egrets)
Size: 38"
Season: Year-round in Florida
Habitat: Fresh- or saltwater marshes

One of our most widespread herons, the Great Egret is all white with a long, thin, yellow bill and long black legs. It develops long, lacy plumes across its back during breeding season. Stalking slowly, it pursues fish, frogs, and other aquatic animals. The illustration shows a breeding adult.

Snowy Egret,
Egretta thula
Family Ardeidae (Herons, Egrets)
Size: 24"
Season: Year-round in Florida
Habitat: Open water, marshes, mangrove swamps

The Snowy Egret is all white with lacy plumes across the back in breeding season. The bill is slim and black, and the legs are black with bright yellow feet. The juvenile has greenish legs with a yellow stripe along the front. It forages for fish and frogs along the shore by moving quickly, shuffling to stir up prey, and stabbing it. Sometimes it may run to pursue its prey. One can remember the name of this bird by thinking that it wears yellow "boots" because it is cold or "snowy." The illustration shows a breeding adult.

Reddish Egret,
Egretta rufescens
Family Ardeidae (Herons, Egrets)
Size: 26"
Season: Year-round in Florida
Habitat: Coastal lagoons

The Reddish Egret is thick-necked and has two color morphs: an all-white version and the more common dark version. The dark morph is gray with a rusty-reddish neck lined with stringy coarse feathers that give it a disheveled look. The bill is long and powerful and pinkish with a black tip. A quite active bird, it often runs through the shallows and chases after fish like a maniac. It also employs the technique of creating an area of shade with its outstretched wings to attract fish and see them better. Usually solitary. The illustration shows an adult.

Tricolored Heron,
Egretta tricolor
Family Ardeidae (Herons, Egrets)
Size: 26"
Season: Year-round in Florida
Habitat: Salt marshes, mangrove swamps

The Tricolored Heron is a thin, bluish-gray heron with a white belly and brownish neck stripe and lower back. In nonbreeding plumage, it has yellow lores and an orangey bill, but in breeding season this area of the lores and bill are blue and the bill has a dark tip. It also develops plumes behind the ears and across the lower back. To feed, it will actively pursue prey or stand motionless, waiting to stab a fish or frog with its thin, spearlike bill. The illustration shows a breeding adult.

Little Blue Heron,
Egretta caerulea
Family Ardeidae (Herons, Egrets)
Size: 25"
Season: Year-round in Florida
Habitat: Freshwater or coastal swamps

The Little Blue Heron is a medium-size heron that skulks along shorelines with vegetative cover, often using its wings to cast a shadow over the water to see and attract fish. It is overall slate blue with a purple cast on the neck. The bill is pale gray with a dark tip, and the legs are greenish. The juvenile is all white with small dark tips on the primaries, and it can be confused with other white herons. The illustration shows an adult.

Cattle Egret, *Bubulcus ibis*
Family Ardeidae (Herons, Egrets)
Size: 20"
Season: Year-round in Florida
Habitat: Upland fields, often near cattle in grazing land

The Cattle Egret is a widespread species originally from Africa and now quite common in the Southeast. Unlike most herons, it is not normally found in aquatic environments. It forms groups around cattle, often perching atop them, and feeds on insects aroused by the movement of their hooves. It is stocky and all white with a comparatively short yellow bill and short black legs. In breeding plumage, the legs and bill turn a bright orange, and a peachy, pale yellow forms on the crown, breast, and back. The illustration shows a nonbreeding adult.

Green Heron,
Butorides virescens
Family Ardeidae (Herons, Egrets)
Size: 18"
Season: Year-round in Florida
Habitat: Ponds, creeks, coastal wetlands (fresh- or saltwater)

The Green Heron is a compact, crow-size heron that perches on low branches over the water, crouching forward to search for fish, snails, and insects. It is known to toss a bug into the water to help attract fish. The Green Heron is really not so green but a dull, grayish-blue with a burgundy-chestnut-colored neck and black crown. The bill is dark and the legs are bright yellow-orange. When disturbed, it will erect its crest feathers, stand erect, and twitch its tail. Fairly secretive and solitary. The illustration shows an adult.

Black-crowned Night-Heron,
Nycticorax nycticorax
Family Ardeidae (Herons, Egrets)
Size: 25"
Season: Year-round in Florida
Habitat: Marshes, swamps with wooded banks

The nocturnal Black-crowned Night-Heron is a stocky, thick-necked heron with a comparatively large head and sharp, heavy, thick bill. It has pale gray wings, white underparts, and black crown, back, and bill. The eyes are piercing red and legs are yellow. In breeding plumage, it develops long, white plumes on the rear of the head. During the day, it roosts in groups, but at night it forages alone, waiting motionless for prey such as fish or crabs. It may even raid the nests of other birds for their young. Its voice is composed of low-pitched barks and croaks. The illustration shows an adult.

Yellow-crowned Night-Heron,
Nyctanassa violacea
Family Ardeidae (Herons, Egrets)
Size: 24"
Season: Year-round in Florida
Habitat: Marshes, ponds, coastal shrubs

Shaped somewhat like the Black-crowned Night-Heron, the Yellow-crowned Night-Heron is blue-gray overall with a black face, white cheek patch, and slim, pale crown that is not really yellow but whitish or pale buff. In breeding plumage, it develops plumes from behind the crest. Its eyes are large and red, and its legs are yellow. The immature bird is drab brown-gray, mottled with light streaks. It is nocturnal but will occasionally feed during the day for crustaceans and other aquatic animals, roosting in groups at night. The illustration shows an adult.

White Ibis, *Eudocimus albus*
Family Threskiornithidae (Ibises, Spoonbills)
Size: 25"
Season: Year-round in Florida
Habitat: Salt marshes, swamps, mangroves, fields

Fairly common in southern Florida, the White Ibis forages in groups, probing the mud and shallow water for small aquatic animals and invertebrates. It is all white except for the black tips of the primaries, which are rarely visible unless the wings are outstretched. The long, downward-curved bill is red with a darker tip and meets the face in unfeathered, reddish-pink facial skin to the eye. Legs are red. The juvenile is dark brown above with a dark, streaky neck. Ibises fly with necks outstretched, unlike herons, which fly with the neck folded back. The illustration shows an adult.

Roseate Spoonbill,
Platalea ajaja
Family Threskiornithidae (Ibises, Spoonbills)
Size: 32"
Season: Year-round in southern Florida
Habitat: Shallow saltwater wetlands, mangrove marshes, agricultural fields

The Roseate Spoonbill is easily identified by its unique feeding technique of swinging its bill from side to side in shallow water or mud for fish, shrimp, and other small aquatic life. Unlike the heron, it constantly moves forward and seldom remains stationary. Its body is pink with red in the shoulders; its neck is white and tail is orange. The face is pale green-gray bordered by a black feathered patch. The bill is very long, thick at the base, and thinning to a compressed, spatula shape. It flies with neck outstretched. While resting, they will stand on one leg for considerable lengths of time. The illustration shows an adult.

Turkey Vulture, *Cathartes aura*
Family Cathartidae (New World Vultures)
Size: 27"
Season: Year-round in Florida
Habitat: Open, dry country

The Turkey Vulture is known for its effortless, skilled soaring. It will often soar for hours without flapping, rocking in the breeze on its long, 6-foot wings that form an upright "V" shape, or dihedral. It has a black body and inner wing with pale flight feathers and tail, which gives it a noticeable two-toned appearance from below. The tail is longish, and the feet extend to no more than halfway past the base of the tail. Its head is naked, red, and small, so the bird appears almost headless in flight. The bill is strongly hooked to aid in tearing apart its favored prey of carrion. Juveniles have a dark gray head. Often roosts in flocks and forms groups around food or at a roadkill site. The illustration shows an adult.

Black Vulture,
Coragyps atratus
Family Cathartidae (New World Vultures)
Size: 25"
Season: Year-round in Florida
Habitat: Open, dry country

Like the Turkey Vulture, the Black Vulture is adept at soaring. Its wing beats, however, are faster, and while soaring, it holds its wings at a flat angle instead of a dihedral. It is stocky in physique, has a short, stubby tail, and shorter wings than the Turkey Vulture. The primaries are pale on an otherwise black body, and the head is bald and gray. It eats carrion and garbage and is quite aggressive at feeding sites. The illustration shows an adult.

Osprey, *Pandion haliaetus*
Family Pandionidae (Osprey)
Size: 23"; female larger than male
Season: Year-round in Florida
Habitat: Always near water,
salt or fresh

Also known as the Fish Hawk, the Osprey exhibits a dramatic feeding method in which it plunges feetfirst into the water to snag fish. Sometimes it may completely submerge itself, and then laboriously fly off with its heavy catch. It is dark brown above, white below, and has a distinct, dark eye stripe contiguous with the nape. Females show a dark, mottled "necklace" across the breast, and juveniles have pale streaking on the back. Ospreys fly with an obvious crook at the wrist, appearing gull-like. Its wings are long and narrow with a dark carpal patch. The illustration shows an adult.

Northern Harrier, *Circus cyaneus*
Family Accipitridae (Raptors)
Size: 18"; female larger than male
Season: Winter in Florida
Habitat: Open fields and wetlands

Also known as the Marsh Hawk, the Northern Harrier flies low to the ground, methodically surveying its hunting grounds for rodents and other small animals. When it spots prey, aided by its acute hearing, it will drop abruptly to the ground to attack. It is a thin raptor with long, flame-shaped wings that are broad in the middle, and a long tail. The face has a distinct, owl-like facial disk and there is a conspicuous white patch at the rump. Males are gray above with a white, streaked breast and black wing tips. Females are brown with a barred breast. The juvenile is similar in plumage to the female but with a pale belly. The illustration shows a female, below, and a male, above.

Snail Kite,
Rostrhamus sociabilis
Family Accipitridae (Raptors)
Size: 17"
Season: Year-round in Florida
Habitat: Freshwater marshes

Also known as the Everglade Kite, the Snail Kite is a tropical species with very specific feeding habits. It relies almost exclusively on a certain "apple snail" that it snatches from the grass while in flight. It then removes the flesh from its shell with its sharply hooked bill and sharp talons. The plumage is dark overall except for the front half of the tail, which is white. Males are dark slate gray with red legs. Females are dark brown with a streaked breast and lighter facial markings. Florida is the only US state in which to find the Snail Kite, and its numbers are very sensitive to habitat changes and the availability of snails. The illustration shows a male, below, and a female, above.

Swallow-tailed Kite,
Elanoides forficatus
Family Accipitridae (Raptors)
Size: 23"
Season: Summer in Florida
Habitat: Wooded environments, wetlands

The Swallow-tailed Kite is a graceful, skilled flier that feeds on the wing, catching insects midair or snatching reptiles from tree branches. It even drinks by skimming along the water surface. It resembles a large swallow with its long, deeply forked tail and long, thin wings. The body and head are white, and the back, tail, and wings are black. The bill is small and hooked, and the eye is dark. May flock together while feeding or during migration to and from its winter home in South America. The illustration shows an adult.

Sharp-shinned Hawk,
Accipiter striatus
Family Accipitridae (Raptors)
Size: 10–14"; female larger than male
Season: Winter in Florida
Habitat: Woodlands, bushy areas

The Sharp-shinned Hawk is our smallest accipiter, with a long-ish, squared tail and stubby, rounded wings. Its short wings allow for agile flight in tight, wooded quarters, where it quickly attacks small birds in flight. It is grayish above and light below, barred with pale rufous. Eyes are set forward on the face to aid in the direct pursuit of prey. The juvenile is white below streaked with brown. Compare it with the larger Cooper's Hawk. The illustration shows an adult.

RAPTORS

Cooper's Hawk,
Accipiter cooperii
Family Accipitridae (Raptors)
Size: 17"; female larger than male
Season: Winter in southern Florida, year-round in northern Florida
Habitat: Woodlands

The Cooper's Hawk perches stealthily and then, on the wing through thickets, ambushes its prey of smaller birds or mammals. Its plumage is very similar to the Sharp-shinned Hawk, although the Cooper's Hawk is larger in size, has a slightly longer, rounded tail, thinner wings, and a relatively larger head. Its eyes are set more in the middle of the face. Unlike the Sharp-shinned Hawk, Cooper's Hawks may perch and hunt in open country. The illustration shows an adult.

Red-shouldered Hawk,
Buteo lineatus
Family Accipitridae (Raptors)
Size: 17"
Season: Year-round in Florida
Habitat: Wooded areas near water

The Red-shouldered Hawk is a solitary, small, accipiter-like buteo with a long tail. It waits patiently on its perch before flying down to attack a variety of small animals. It has a banded black-and-white tail and spotted dark wings. The head and shoulder are rust-colored, while the breast is light with rust barring. Its legs are long and yellow and its bill is hooked. In flight there is a pale arc just inside the wing tips, and it flaps with quick wing beats followed by short glides. The Florida population is much paler overall than its western counterparts. The illustration shows an adult, Florida race.

Short-tailed Hawk,
Buteo brachyurus
Family Accipitridae (Raptors)
Size: 16"
Season: Year-round in southern Florida
Habitat: Forest or mixed woodland/ grassland

The reclusive Short-tailed Hawk is a smallish, plump buteo with rounded wings and a short tail. The slim forehead runs contiguous with the upper bill, giving a flat-headed appearance. Two color morphs exist: The dark morph, more common in Florida, is dark brown overall with light wing linings, and the light morph has clean white underparts. In flight, it holds its wings flat with the tips bending up. To feed, it kites above the treetops and plunges to capture prey. Florida is the only state in which to find this tropical species in the United States. The illustration shows an adult dark morph.

Red-tailed Hawk,
Buteo jamaicensis
Family Accipitridae (Raptors)
Size: 20"
Season: Year-round in Florida
Habitat: Telephone poles, posts near open country, prairies

This widespread species is the most common buteo in the United States. It has broad, rounded wings and a stout hooked bill. Its plumage is highly variable depending on geographic location. In general the underparts are light with darker streaking that forms a dark band across the belly, the upperparts are dark brown, and the tail is rufous. Light spotting occurs along the scapulars. In flight there is a noticeable dark patch along the inner leading edge of the underwing. Red-tailed Hawks glide down from a perch to catch rodents, and they may hover to spot prey. Usually seen alone or in pairs, its voice is the familiar *keeer!* The illustration shows an adult.

Bald Eagle,
Haliaeetus leucocephalus
Family Accipitridae (Raptors)
Size: 30–40"; female larger than male
Season: Year-round in Florida
Habitat: Seashores, lakes, rivers with tall perches or cliffs

The Bald Eagle is a large raptor that is widespread but fairly uncommon. It eats fish or scavenges dead animals and may congregate in large numbers where food is abundant. Its plumage is dark brown contrasting with a white head and tail. Juveniles show white splotching across the wings and breast. The yellow bill is large and powerful, and the talons are large and sharp. In flight it holds its wings fairly flat and straight, resembling a long plank. Bald Eagles make huge nests of sticks high in trees. The illustration shows an adult.

Crested Caracara,
Caracara cheriway
Family Falconidae (Falcons)
Size: 23"
Season: Year-round in Florida
Habitat: Dry prairies and scrubland

The Northern Caracara is a falcon that is somewhat vulturelike in its behavior. It forages on carcasses or immobile prey, which it finds by soaring on flat wings or cruising over pastures and open savanna. It may also perch on poles or on the ground. Its head seems large for its body, and it has a long neck and long legs. It is an overall dark bird with a white neck, black cap, and large, hooked bill. The face has a large patch of reddish bare skin. In flight the white wing tips and tail are distinctive. This tropical falcon is rare in the United States and was once a threatened species here. The illustration shows an adult.

American Kestrel, *Falco sparverius*
Family Falconidae (Falcons)
Size: 10"
Season: Year-round in Florida
Habitat: Branches or wires in open country, urban areas

Our most common falcon, the American Kestrel, is a tiny, robin-size falcon with long, pointed wings and tail and fast flight. It hovers above fields or dives from its perch to capture small animals and insects. Its upperparts are rufous barred with black, its wings are blue-gray, and its breast is buffy or white streaked with black spots. The head is patterned with a gray crown and vertical patches of black down the face. The female has rufous wings and a barred tail. Also known as the Sparrow Hawk, it has a habit of flicking its tail up and down while perched. The illustration shows an adult male.

Common Moorhen,
Gallinula chloropus
Family Rallidae (Rails, Coots)
Size: 14"
Season: Year-round in Florida
Habitat: Freshwater ponds and wetlands

The Common Moorhen, like the Coot, is actually a type of rail that behaves more like a duck. It paddles along, bobbing its head up and down, picking at the water surface for any small aquatic animals, insects, or plants. Having short wings, it is a poor flier, but its very long toes allow it to walk on floating vegetation. It is overall dark gray with a brownish back, black head, and white areas on the tail and sides. In breeding plumage, the forehead shield is deep red and the bill is red with a yellow tip. Also known as the Common Gallinule. The illustration shows a breeding adult.

American Coot, *Fulica americana*
Family Rallidae (Rails, Coots)
Size: 15"
Season: Year-round in Florida
Habitat: Wetlands, ponds, urban lawns, and parks

The American Coot is a rail like the Moorhen, but with a plumper body and thicker head and neck. It is a very common bird and becomes relatively tame in urban areas and parks. To feed, it dives for fish but will also dabble like a duck or pick food from the ground. It is dark gray overall with a black head and a white bill that ends with a narrow dark ring. In flight one can see the white trailing edge of the wings. The toes are flanked with lobes that enable walking on water plants and efficient swimming. Juveniles are similar in plumage but paler. Coots are often seen in very large flocks. The illustration shows an adult.

Clapper Rail, *Rallus longirostris*
Family Rallidae (Rails, Coots)
Size: 14"
Season: Year-round in Florida
Habitat: Coastal saltwater or
brackish marshes, mangrove swamps

Also known as the Marsh Hen, the Clapper Rail is very shy and difficult to see. It lurks through marshy vegetation and usually chooses to walk or swim rather than fly. It forages by probing through mud and grass for a variety of small prey, vocalizing harsh, clattering *kek-kek-kek* sounds in rapid succession. It is a relatively thin rail with a long, slightly decurved bill. The plumage is gray-brown above with a pale rust breast and barred flanks. The illustration shows an adult.

Limpkin, *Aramus guarauna*
Family Aramidae (Limpkin)
Size: 26"
Season: Year-round in Florida
Habitat: Shallow wetlands with
vegetation

Named for its slow walking gait, which resembles a limp, the Limpkin looks somewhat like a small crane. It has a long neck, long legs, and a long, decurving bill. Its plumage is dark brown with white streaking down the head and neck and onto the front half of the body. In flight it holds the neck extended below the body creating a humpbacked appearance. Limpkins forage by walking steadily or swimming, picking out mollusk, apple snails, and other aquatic invertebrates. Its voice is a loud, raucous call. The illustration shows an adult.

Sandhill Crane, *Grus canadensis*
Family Gruidae (Cranes)
Size: 45"
Season: Year-round in Florida
Habitat: Fields, shallow wetlands, savanna

The Sandhill Crane is tall bird with long, strong legs, a long neck, and a long, straight bill. The long, thick, tertial feathers create the distinctive bustle on the rear of all cranes. The top of the head is covered by red, bare skin. Plumage is gray overall but may become spotted with rust-colored stains by preening with a bill stained by iron-rich mud. In flocks, it grazes in fields gleaning grains, insects, and small animals, returning in the evening to roost in protected wetland areas. The voice of the Sandhill Crane is a throaty, penetrating, trumpeting sound. Unlike the heron, it flies in groups with the neck extended. The Florida population is nonmigratory and larger than northern races. The illustration shows an adult.

Black-bellied Plover,
Pluvialis squatarola
Family Charadriidae (Plovers)
Size: 11"
Season: Winter in Florida
Habitat: Open areas, coastal or inland

The Black-bellied Plover is a relatively large plover with long, pointed wings and a whistling flight call. Like other plovers, it feeds by scooting quickly along the ground and stopping suddenly to peck at small prey in the mud or sand, and then scooting along again. Its winter plumage is gray above and paler below with a white belly. The bill is short, black, and thick. In flight there is a distinctive black patch on the axillary feathers. In breeding plumage, it develops the sharply contrasting black belly, face, and front of the neck. The illustration shows a breeding adult, below, and a nonbreeding adult, above.

Semipalmated Plover,
Charadrius semipalmatus
Family Charadriidae (Plovers)
Size: 7"
Season: Winter in Florida
Habitat: Open sand or mudflats, coastal beaches

The Semipalmated Plover is a small, plump plover with pointed wings, large black eyes, and a relatively large, rounded head. It has a dark brown back and crown, is white below, and has a small, orange bill with a dark tip. The head has dark bands across the eye and encircling the neck. Legs and feet are yellow. Winter and breeding plumages are similar with the exception of an all-dark bill and lighter supercilium in winter. This widespread plover flies in flocks but disperses to feed, when it uses fast running interrupted by sudden stops to probe for invertebrates. Its name is derived from the partial webbing at the base of its toes. The illustration shows a breeding adult.

Wilson's Plover,
Charadrius wilsonia
Family Charadriidae (Plovers)
Size: 8"
Season: Year-round in Florida
Habitat: Drier areas of coastal sandy beaches and flats

The Wilson's Plover resembles the Semipalmated Plover but has shorter wings and a much longer bill. This tropical species is quite solitary and slow-moving, feeding mostly at night on insects, crabs, and coastal invertebrates. It is brownish-gray on the back and head with a pale streak above the eye and a white forehead, chin, and belly. Legs are dull pink. A dark ring encircles the neck, which becomes black in breeding plumage. The illustration shows a breeding adult.

Killdeer, *Charadrius vociferus*
Family Charadriidae (Plovers)
Size: 10"
Season: Year-round in Florida
Habitat: Inland fields, farmlands, lake shores, meadows

The Killdeer gets its name from the piercing *kill-dee* call that one often hears before seeing this well-camouflaged plovers. Well adapted to human-altered environments, it is quite widespread and gregarious. It has long, pointed wings, a long tail, and a conspicuous double-banded breast. Its upper parts are dark brown, its belly is white, and its head is patterned with a white supercilium and forehead. The tail is rusty orange with a black tip. In flight there is a noticeable white stripe across the flight feathers. The Killdeer is known for the classic "broken wing" display, which it uses to distract predators from its nest and young. The illustration shows an adult.

American Oystercatcher,
Haematopus palliatus
Family Haematopodidae (Oystercatchers)
Size: 18"
Season: Year-round in Florida
Habitat: Coastal beaches, tide pools

The American Oystercatcher is a chunky, short-tailed, and short-winged shorebird with a dark brown back, white belly, and black head. It has a heavy, knifelike, bright red bill, yellow eyes, and stocky, salmon-colored legs. In flight there is a distinct white bar across the secondary feathers. It follows the tidal pattern, foraging at low tide and roosting at high tide in groups with other shorebirds and gulls. It uses its bill to pry away shellfish—including oysters—from rocks, or to probe for worms. The bill is also used to jam open bivalves and devour the flesh. Its voice is a loud, piping call. The illustration shows an adult.

American Avocet,
Recurvirostra americana
Family Recurvirostridae (Avocets, Stilts)
Size: 18"
Season: Winter in Florida
Habitat: Shallow wetlands, marshes, coastal lagoons

The elegant American Avocet has a long, delicate, black, upturned bill, and long, thin, blue-gray legs. The upperparts are patterned black and white, the belly is white, and the head and neck are light orange-brown punctuated by black eyes. The bill of the female is slightly shorter with a greater bend than that of the male. Nonbreeding adults have a pale gray head and neck. Avocets use a side-to-side sweeping motion with the bill to stir up small crustaceans and insect larvae as they wade methodically through the shallows. They may even submerge their head as the water deepens. They are adept swimmers and emit a *wheet!* call in alarm. The illustration shows a breeding male, below, and a non-breeding female, above.

Black-necked Stilt,
Himantopus mexicanus
Family Recurvirostridae (Avocets, Stilts)
Size: 14"
Season: Year-round in Florida
Habitat: Shallow wetlands, marshes, lagoons

The Black-necked Stilt literally looks like a tiny body on stilts. It has extremely long, delicate, red legs, and a thin, straight, needle-like, black bill. Wings and mantle are black and the underparts and tail are white. The head is dark above with a white patch above the eye. The female has a slightly lighter, brownish back. In flight the long legs dangle behind the bird. To forage, it strides along to pick small prey from the water or vegetation and may voice a strident, barking *kek* in alarm. Stilts are also known to perform the broken-wing or broken-leg act to distract predators. The illustration shows an adult male.

Greater Yellowlegs,
Tringa melanoleuca
Family Scolopacidae (Sandpipers)
Size: 14"
Season: Winter in Florida
Habitat: Salt- or freshwater marshes

The Greater Yellowlegs is sometimes called the "tell-tale" bird, as it is the sentinel of a flock that raises alarm when danger is near, flying off and circling to return. It has long, bright yellow legs, a long neck, a dark, slightly upturned bill, and a white eye ring. Its upperparts are dark gray and mottled, while its underparts are white with barring on the flanks. In breeding plumage, the barring is noticeably darker and more extensive. To feed, it strides forward actively to pick up small aquatic prey or chase fish. The Lesser Yellowlegs is similar but smaller. The illustration shows a nonbreeding adult.

Willet, **Tringa** *semipalmatus*
Family Scolopacidae (Sandpipers)
Size: 15"
Season: Year-round in Florida
Habitat: Salt- or freshwater wetlands

The Willet is a heavy shorebird with a stout bill and conspicuous black-and-white wing markings in flight. It has overall mocha-brown plumage above and pale below with extensive mottling in the breeding season. It has white lores and eye ring, and its plain gray legs are thick and sturdy. It is found singly or in scattered flocks and picks or probes for crabs, other crustaceans, and worms in the mud and sand. Its call is a loud *wil-let* often uttered in flight. The illustration shows a nonbreeding adult.

Spotted Sandpiper,
Actitus macularius
Family Scolopacidae (Sandpipers)
Size: 7.5"
Season: Winter in Florida
Habitat: Creek sides, edges of lakes and ponds

The solitary Spotted Sandpiper is known for its exaggerated, constant bobbing motion. It has a compact body, long tail, and a short neck and legs. Its plumage is brown above and light below with a white shoulder patch. There is a white eye ring and superciliary stripe above a dark eye line. In breeding plumage, it develops heavy spotting from the chin to the lower flanks, and barring on the back. The bill is orange with a dark tip. In flight its short wings and the thin white stripe on the upper wing can be seen. To forage, it teeters about picking for small water prey and insects along the shoreline. The illustration shows a breeding adult.

Whimbrel, *Numenius phaeopus*
Family Scolopacidae (Sandpipers)
Size: 17"
Season: Winter in Florida
Habitat: Coastal wetlands, farmlands

Also known as the Hudsonian Curlew, the Whimbrel is a large shorebird with a very long, decurved bill. It is overall gray-brown, and paler beneath with barring. The head has a dark eye stripe and cap with a pale central crown stripe. Its legs are dark gray. Plumages in all seasons are similar. It forages singly or in small groups, probing or picking with its long, sensitive bill, searching for invertebrates and coaxing fiddler crabs from their burrows. Call is a soft *ker-loo*. The illustration shows an adult.

Long-billed Curlew,
Numenius americanus
Family Scolopacidae (Sandpipers)
Size: 23"
Season: Winter in Florida
Habitat: Open grasslands, coastal mudflats, and beaches

Sometimes called the "Sicklebill," the Long-billed Curlew is our largest curlew with and extremely long, thin, decurved bill (longer in females than in males). It is mottled gray-brown above with buff underparts. Facial markings are not pronounced, and the underside of the wings is a rich cinnamon color. It strides ahead in a deliberate manner with head forward, picking or probing for crustaceans and insects. Its large eyes enable it to feed in the dark hours of early morning. Its voice is a loud, ringing *kur-lee!* May form flocks with Whimbrels and Godwits during the winter months. The illustration shows an adult.

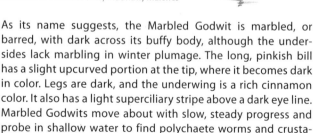

Marbled Godwit, *Limosa fedoa*
Family Scolopacidae (Sandpipers)
Size: 18"
Season: Most seasons except summer in Florida
Habitat: Coastal beaches, mudflats, marshes

As its name suggests, the Marbled Godwit is marbled, or barred, with dark across its buffy body, although the undersides lack marbling in winter plumage. The long, pinkish bill has a slight upcurved portion at the tip, where it becomes dark in color. Legs are dark, and the underwing is a rich cinnamon color. It also has a light superciliary stripe above a dark eye line. Marbled Godwits move about with slow, steady progress and probe in shallow water to find polychaete worms and crustaceans. Its call is a loud *god-WIT*. The illustration shows a non-breeding adult.

Ruddy Turnstone, *Arenaria interpres*
Family Scolopacidae (Sandpipers)
Size: 9.5"
Season: Predominantly winter in Florida, although may be found year-round
Habitat: Wide variety of shoreline habitats, rocky intertidal to beaches and mudflats

The gregarious and frenetic Ruddy Turnstone is a chunky, short-legged shorebird with a short, wedge-shaped bill. The breeding adult has ruddy and black upperparts, a white belly, and a complex pattern of black and white on the head. The nonbreeding bird is pale brown and black above with drab head markings. The stubby legs are orange. In flight the bird is white below and strongly patterned light and dark above. Turnstones bustle about constantly to pick, pry, or probe for almost any food item. Indeed, it will "turn stones" to search for prey. The illustration shows a breeding adult, below, and a nonbreeding adult, above.

Red Knot, *Calidris canutus*
Family Scolopacidae (Sandpipers)
Size: 10.5"
Season: Primarily winter in Florida
Habitat: Coastal beaches and mudflats

The Red Knot is a compact, short-legged shorebird with a slightly down-curved bill. In Florida we mostly see it in nonbreeding plumage, which is mottled gray-brown above and pale below with light streaking. In breeding plumage, it has a rufous body with a grayish back and wings. The bill is dark, about the length of the head. In flight the long, pointed wings, which are gray underneath, can be seen. It forages by probing and picking in the mud or sand for a variety of small prey. Often forms tight flocks while roosting and feeding. The illustration shows a breeding adult, below, and a nonbreeding adult, above.

Sanderling, *Calidris alba*
Family Scolopacidae (Sandpipers)
Size: 8"
Season: Winter in Florida
Habitat: Coastal beaches, mudflats

The Sanderling is a common shorebird that runs back and forth following the incoming and outgoing surf, grabbing invertebrates exposed by the waves. It is a small, active, squat sandpiper with a short bill and legs. In nonbreeding plumage, it is very pale above and white below, which contrasts with its black legs and bill. There is a distinct black shoulder and leading edge on the wing. Females in breeding plumage are speckled brown above, while males develop rufous on the back, head, and neck. In flight one sees a white wing stripe on the upper wing. Sanderlings may form large foraging flocks and even larger flocks while roosting. The illustration shows a nonbreeding adult.

Dunlin, *Calidris alpina*
Family Scolopacidae (Sandpipers)
Size: 8.5"
Season: Winter in Florida
Habitat: Coastal beaches, mudflats

The name "Dunlin" comes from the word "dun," which means a dull, gray-brown color, and which describes the winter plumage of this bird. It is a rather small sandpiper with a long bill that droops down at the tip. In breeding plumage, there is a black belly patch and rufous tones on the back. In flight one sees a white wing stripe on the upper wing and a white rump separated by a central dark line. It forms huge flocks, swirling and circling in unison. To feed, it walks steadily through shallow waters probing and picking crustaceans and other invertebrates. The illustration shows a breeding adult, below, and a nonbreeding adult, above.

Western Sandpiper,
Calidris mauri
Family Scolopacidae (Sandpipers)
Size: 6.5"
Season: Winter in Florida
Habitat: Salt- or freshwater wetlands, mudflats

The Western Sandpiper is one of the "peeps," or very small sandpipers. It has a relatively long, black bill that droops slightly, and black legs. In winter it is pale gray-brown above and white below. In breeding plumage, there is rufous on the scapulars and face, and much darker streaking on the breast and back. In flight there is a thin white stripe on the upper wing and a white rump with a dark, central stripe. Western Sandpipers feed in shallow water or at the tideline, probing or picking invertebrates and insects. They often form rather large flocks. The illustration shows a breeding adult, below, and a nonbreeding adult, above.

Common Snipe, *Gallinago gallinago*
Family Scolopacidae (Sandpipers)
Size: 10.5"
Season: Winter in Florida
Habitat: Salt- or freshwater marshes

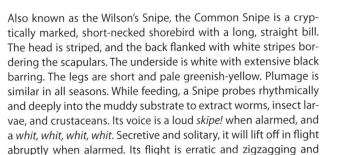

Also known as the Wilson's Snipe, the Common Snipe is a cryptically marked, short-necked shorebird with a long, straight bill. The head is striped, and the back flanked with white stripes bordering the scapulars. The underside is white with extensive black barring. The legs are short and pale greenish-yellow. Plumage is similar in all seasons. While feeding, a Snipe probes rhythmically and deeply into the muddy substrate to extract worms, insect larvae, and crustaceans. Its voice is a loud *skipe!* when alarmed, and a *whit, whit, whit, whit*. Secretive and solitary, it will lift off in flight abruptly when alarmed. Its flight is erratic and zigzagging and includes "winnowing," a display where air across the tail feathers whistles during a steep descent. The illustration shows an adult.

Bonaparte's Gull,
Chroicocephalus philadelphia
Family Laridae (Gulls, Terns)
Size: 13"
Season: Winter in Florida
Habitat: Coastal in winter, comes inland during migration

The Bonaparte's Gull is a small gull named for the American ornithologist who was related to Napoleon. It is agile and tern-like in flight, skimming low over the water to snatch fish. It has a thin, sharp, black bill and red legs. Plumage in breeding season includes a black head that contrasts with its white body and light gray back and wings. The primaries form a white triangle against the dark trailing edge in flight. The nonbreeding adult has a mostly white head with a black eye and a small dark spot around the ear. A solitary gull, it does not form large flocks, and its nest is made of sticks in evergreen trees. The illustration shows a breeding adult, below, and a nonbreeding adult, above.

Laughing Gull, *Leucophaeus atricilla*
Family Laridae (Gulls, Terns)
Size: 16"
Season: Year-round in Florida
Habitat: Coastal beaches and marshes, urban environments, pastures

The Laughing Gull is so named because of its loud, often incessant, laughing squawk and is the only gull known to breed in Florida. Social and uninhibited, it is a relatively thin, medium-size gull with long, pointed wings. The breeding adult has a black head with white eye arcs and a dark red bill. Upperparts are dark gray, underparts are white, and wing tips are black with small white dots at the ends. The nonbreeding adult has a white head with faint dark smudging behind the eye. Laughing Gulls eat crabs, fish, and worms and will scavenge from humans for food or even steal from other birds. The illustration shows a breeding adult, below, and a nonbreeding adult, above.

Ring-billed Gull, *Larus delewarensis*
Family Laridae (Gulls, Terns)
Size: 18"
Season: Winter in Florida
Habitat: Widespread from coast to inland lakes and ponds, parking lots

The Ring-billed Gull is common and quite tame. It is a relatively small gull with a rounded, white head and a yellow bill with a dark subterminal ring. It has a pale gray back with black primaries tipped with white and white underparts. Its eye is pale yellow; its legs are yellow. The nonbreeding adult has faint streaking on the nape and around the eye. Ring-billed Gulls feed from the water or on the ground, taking a wide variety of food, and may scavenge in urban areas and dumps. The illustration shows a nonbreeding adult.

Herring Gull, *Larus argentatus*
Family Laridae (Gulls, Terns)
Size: 25"
Season: Winter in Florida
Habitat: Widespread, mainly coastal, but may travel inland; beaches, harbors, fields

The widespread Herring Gull occurs across the North American continent. It is a large, relatively thin, white-headed gull with a pale gray back and white underparts. The bill is thick and yellow with a reddish spot at the tip of the lower mandible. The primaries are black with white-spotted tips. The nonbreeding adult has brown streaking across the nape and neck. The legs are pink and the eye is pale yellow to ivory colored. The Ring-billed Gull is an opportunistic feeder, eating fish, worms, crumbs, and trash. It is known to drop shellfish from the air to crack open their shells. The illustration shows a breeding adult, below, and a nonbreeding adult, above.

GULLS, TERNS

Caspian Tern, *Hydroprogne caspia*
Family Laridae (Gulls, Terns)
Size: 21"
Season: Year-round in Florida
Habitat: Coastal and inland
lakes and rivers

The Caspian Tern is a very large, thick-necked tern, the size of a large gull. It has a rich, red, pointed bill that is dark at the tip. The upperparts are very pale gray, the underparts are white, and the head has a black cap. The primary feathers are pale gray above and tipped with dark on the underside. The legs are short and black. The nonbreeding adult has pale streaks through the cap. In flight the Caspian Tern uses ponderous, shallow wing beats and is less agile than smaller terns. It flies above the water surface searching for small fish, plunging headfirst to snatch prey, and may rob food from other birds. Its voice is a harsh *craw!* The illustration shows a breeding adult.

Royal Tern, *Thalasseus maxima*
Family Laridae (Gulls, Terns)
Size: 20"
Season: Year-round in Florida
Habitat: Coastal beaches, salt marshes

The Royal Tern is a large but sleek tern with pointed, thin wings, a black, crested cap, and a red-orange, pointed bill. It is pale gray above and white below with black legs. The nonbreeding adult has limited dark on the head, often reduced to a dark patch just behind the eye. The dark outer primaries are visible in flight. Like the Caspian Tern, the Royal Tern flies over the water surface, often hovering, and then plunging down to catch fish. It breeds on sandbars in the company of thousands of other birds. The illustration shows a breeding adult, below, and a nonbreeding adult, above.

Least Tern, *Sternula antillarum*
Family Laridae (Gulls, Terns)
Size: 9"
Season: Summer in Florida
Habitat: Sandy coastal shores

The Least Tern is the smallest North American tern and the only tern with a yellow bill and legs. It has a black cap and white forehead patch, is pale gray above, and white below. The tail is forked, and the bill tipped with black. Nonbreeding adults have a dark bill and increased white on the front of the cap. In flight the wings are relatively narrow and there is a black bar on the outer primaries. Least Terns often hover over the water before plunge-diving to catch small fish. They also pick worms and insects from the ground. This sensitive bird was once threatened by development of its coastal, sandy breeding grounds. The illustration shows a breeding adult.

Sooty Tern, *Onychoprion fuscata*
Family Laridae (Gulls, Terns)
Size: 16"
Season: Summer in Florida
Habitat: Gulf Coast, Florida Keys, pelagic areas

Worldwide, the Sooty Tern is quite common and gregarious, forming huge breeding colonies. It has a dark, sooty-black back and white underparts with a white forehead patch. The bill is small and black, and the legs are black. The deeply forked tail is black with white outer tail feathers. The nonbreeding adult shows pale mottling on the nape and forehead. Juveniles are all dark with white spotting on the back and wings. Sooty Terns do not usually dive like most terns but drop down to the water surface to catch fish or squid, and may alight on floating objects without swimming. Illustration shows a breeding adult.

Black Skimmer, *Rynchops niger*
Family Laridae (Gulls, Terns)
Size: 18"
Season: Year-round in Florida
Habitat: Coastal bays, estuaries, or inland freshwater rivers and lakes

The Black Skimmer has a most unique bill, in that the lower mandible is substantially longer than the upper. The red bill is also thick at the base and knife-thin toward the end. This aids in the foraging practice of flying just above the water surface, wings held above the body, with the mouth open and the lower mandible cutting a furrow through the water. When it encounters something solid, the mouth slams shut and, hopefully, the bird acquires a fish. Plumage is black on the back, wings, and crown, and white below. The legs are tiny and red. Nonbreeding adults have a white nape, contiguous with the white of the body. The illustration shows a breeding adult.

Mourning Dove, *Zenaida macroura*
Family Columbidae (Pigeons, Doves)
Size: 12"
Season: Year-round in Florida
Habitat: Open brushy area, urban areas

The common Mourning Dove is a sleek, long-tailed dove with a thin neck, a small, rounded head, and a large, black eye. Underneath it is pale gray-brown and darker above with some iridescence to feathers on the neck. There are clear, black spots on the tertials and some coverts, and a dark spot on the upper neck below the eye. The pointed tail is edged with a white band. The Mourning Dove pecks on the ground for seeds and grains, and walks with quick, short steps while bobbing its head. Flight is strong and direct, and the wings create a whistle as the bird takes off. Its voice is a mournful, owl-like cooing. It is usually solitary or found in small groups, but may form large flocks where food is abundant. The illustration shows an adult.

PIGEONS, DOVES

Eurasian Collared-Dove,

Streptopelia decaocto
Family Columbidae (Pigeons, Doves)
Size: 12.5"
Season: Year-round in Florida
Habitat: Human-altered environments,
pastures, rooftops

The Eurasian Collared-Dove was introduced to the United States from Europe and is gradually increasing its numbers here. It is a stocky, fairly large dove with a squarish tail. Plumage is light brown-gray overall with darker primaries, white along the outer edges of the tail, with a contrasting black streak around the nape. The eye is red and the bill is black. In appearance, it is very similar to the smaller, paler Ringed Turtle-Dove. It eats mainly seeds and grain. The illustration shows an adult.

Rock Dove (Pigeon),

Columba livia
Family Columbidae (Pigeons, Doves)
Size: 12"
Season: Year-round in Florida
Habitat: Urban areas, farmland

The Rock Dove is the common pigeon we see in almost every urban area across the continent. Introduced from Europe, where they inhabit rocky cliffs, Rock Doves here have adapted to city life, and domestication has supplied a huge variety of plumage colors and patterns. The original, wild version is a stocky, gray bird with a darker head and neck, and green to purple iridescence along the sides of the neck. The eye is bright red, and the bill has a fleshy, white cere on the base of the upper mandible. There are two dark bars across the back when the wing is folded, the rump is white, and the tail has a dark terminal band. Variants range from white to brown to black, with many pattern combinations. The illustration shows an adult.

PIGEONS, DOVES

White-crowned Pigeon,
Patagioenas leucocephala
Family Columbidae (Pigeons, Doves)
Size: 13"
Season: Year-round in southern Florida along the Keys
Habitat: Forested areas, mangroves

The White-crowned Pigeon is a Caribbean species that is rare and threatened in Florida. It forages among trees for seeds and fruit, voicing its deep, cooing call. It is a large pigeon with short, rounded wings. The body is dark, slate gray with a white crown extending just below the white eye, and the nape is barred with iridescent feathers. The bill is red with a pale tip. In juvenile birds, the white cap is absent. The illustration shows an adult.

Monk Parakeet, *Myiopsitta monachus*
Family Psittacidae (Parrots)
Size: 11"
Season: Year-round in Florida
Habitat: Urban areas

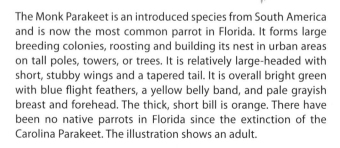

The Monk Parakeet is an introduced species from South America and is now the most common parrot in Florida. It forms large breeding colonies, roosting and building its nest in urban areas on tall poles, towers, or trees. It is relatively large-headed with short, stubby wings and a tapered tail. It is overall bright green with blue flight feathers, a yellow belly band, and pale grayish breast and forehead. The thick, short bill is orange. There have been no native parrots in Florida since the extinction of the Carolina Parakeet. The illustration shows an adult.

Budgerigar,
Melopsittacus undulatus
Family Psittacidae (Parrots)
Size: 7"
Season: Year-round in Florida
Habitat: Urban areas,
telephone wires

The Budgerigar is the familiar bird known simply as "parakeet" in most pet stores. Originally from Australia, it has established populations here from escaped captive birds and is seen in urban areas. It is a small parakeet with a long, tapered tail. The plumage is variable, but the most common form is green below with yellow above, streaked with darker bars. In flight it shows a distinctive yellow stripe along the mid-wing. Its voice is a warbling call. The illustration shows an adult.

Mangrove Cuckoo,
Coccyzus minor
Family Cuculidae (Cuckoos)
Size: 12"
Season: Year-round in Florida
Habitat: Mangrove forests,
hardwood hammocks, or scrub

The shy Mangrove Cuckoo skulks among trees picking out insects and caterpillars while voicing its nasal call of *gaw-gaw-gaw-gaw*. It is brown above and whitish to cinnamon-buff below, and the gray cap on the head is darkest just behind the eye. The bill is two-toned, with the upper mandible gray and the lower mandible yellow. The underside of the long, gradated tail is black with big white spots. The illustration shows an adult.

Yellow-billed Cuckoo,
Coccyzus americanus
Family Cuculidae (Cuckoos)
Size: 12"
Season: Summer in Florida
Habitat: A variety of woodlands,
streamsides, swamps

Like other cuckoos, the Yellow-billed Cuckoo is secretive and shy,
hiding in vegetation where it picks insects, caterpillars, and fruit
from trees. It is brown above with rufous flight feathers and crisp
white below. The bill is yellow with black along the top ridge. The
tail is long and gradated with large white spots on the underside.
The illustration shows an adult.

Smooth-billed Ani,
Croptophaga ani
Family Cuculidae (Cuckoos)
Size: 14"
Season: Year-round in Florida
Habitat: Open fields, grasslands,
urban areas

The fairly rare but social Smooth-billed Ani is a grackle-size, scruffy
black bird that often appears hunched or holds its wings and tail
at odd angles. Its bill is large and laterally compressed, with the
top mandible being much larger that the lower, and with a thin
keel at the top edge. Plumage is black and tinged with brown on
the head and neck and blue-green along the back, wings, and tail.
It picks insects, fruit, and small reptiles or amphibians from the
ground or branches. Its call is a questioning *wa-eek?* The illustration shows an adult.

Great Horned Owl,
Bubo virginianus
Family Strigidae (Typical Owls)
Size: 22"
Season: Year-round in Florida
Habitat: Almost any environment; forests to plains to urban areas

Found throughout North America, the Great Horned Owl is a large, strong owl with an obvious facial disk and sharp, long talons. Plumage is variable, but eastern forms are brown overall with heavy barring, a rust-colored face, and a white chin patch. The prominent ear tufts give the owl its name, and the eyes are large and yellow. The Great Horned Owl has exceptional hearing and sight. It feeds at night, perching on branches or posts and then swooping down on silent wings to catch birds, snakes, or mammals up to the size of a cat. Its voice is a low *hoo-hoo-hoo*. The illustration shows an adult.

TYPICAL OWLS

Barred Owl, *Strix varia*
Family Strigidae (Typical Owls)
Size: 21"
Season: Year-round in Florida
Habitat: Wooded swamps, upland forests

The Barred Owl is a large, compact owl with a short tail and wings, rounded head, and big, dark eyes. It lacks the ear tufts seen on the Great Horned Owl and has comparatively small talons. Plumage is gray-brown overall with dark barring on the neck and breast, turning to streaking on the belly and flanks. It swoops from its perch to catch small rodents, frogs, or snakes. Its voice, often heard during the day, is a hooting, *who-cooks-for-you,* or a kind of bark. Its nests are made in tree cavities vacated by other species. The illustration shows an adult.

Burrowing Owl,
Athene cunicularia
Family Strigidae (Typical Owls)
Size: 9.5"
Season: Year-round in Florida
Habitat: Open grasslands and plains

The Burrowing Owl is a ground-dwelling owl that lives in the burrows that have been vacated by rodents or tortoises. It is small, flat-headed, and has a short tail and long legs. Plumage is brown above spotted with white and extensively barred brown and white below. It has a white chin and throat and bright yellow eyes. The Florida variety is darker and more barred than western counterparts. Burrowing Owls can be seen during the day or night perched on the ground or a post, scanning for insects and small rodents. Sometimes they exhibit a bowing movement when approached. The Burrowing Owl's voice is a chattering or cooing, and sometimes imitative of a rattlesnake. The illustration shows an adult.

Eastern Screech-Owl, *Megascops asio*
Family Strigidae (Typical Owls)
Size: 8.5"
Season: Year-round in Florida
Habitat: Wooded areas or parks,
places where cavity-bearing trees exist

The Eastern Screech Owl is a small, big-headed, eared owl with a short tail and bright yellow eyes. The highly camouflaged plumage ranges from reddish to brown to gray, depending on the region, but the red form is most common in the East. It is darker above, streaked and barred below. The ear tufts may be drawn back to give a rounded head appearance, and the bill is grayish-green tipped with white. White spots on the margins of the coverts and scapulars create two white bars on the folded wing. It is a nocturnal bird, hunting during the night for small mammals, insects, or fish. Its voice is a descending, whistling call or a rapid staccato of one pitch. The illustration shows a red morph adult.

Chuck-will's-widow, *Caprimulgus carolinensis*
Family Caprimulgidae (Nightjars, Nighthawks)
Size: 12"
Season: Year-round in Florida
Habitat: Woodland areas with clearings

Chuck-will's-widow is a highly camouflaged, fairly large nightjar with a fat head, big, dark eyes, and a tiny bill. The body is thick and broad around the midsection, giving a hunched appearance. It is overall rusty or brown-gray, spotted and streaked with black. There are pale edges to the scapulars and a pale chin stripe above the dark breast. The tail is long and projects beyond the primaries. In flight note the long, pointed wings and white on the outer tail feathers in the male. Chuck-will's-widow is nocturnal, feeding at night by springing from its perch or the ground for flying insects. During the day it roosts on the ground or in trees with its eyes closed. Its voice is somewhat like its name, *chuck-wil-wi-dow*. The illustration shows an adult.

Common Nighthawk,
Chordeiles minor
Family Caprimulgidae (Nightjars, Nighthawks)
Size: 9"
Season: Summer in Florida
Habitat: Variety of habitats; forests, marshes, plains, urban areas

The Common Nighthawk is primarily nocturnal but may often be seen flying during the day and evening hours, catching insects on the wing with bounding flight. It is cryptically mottled gray, brown, and black, with strong barring on an otherwise pale underside. In the male, a white breast band is evident. The tail is long and slightly notched, and the wings are long and pointed, extending past the tail in the perched bird. In flight there is a distinct white patch on both sides of the wings. During the day, it is usually seen roosting on posts or branches with its eyes closed. Its voice is a short, nasal, buzzing sound. The illustration shows an adult male.

Chimney Swift,
Chaetura pelagica
Family Apodidae (Swifts)
Size: 5"
Season: Summer in Florida
Habitat: Variety of habitats; woods, scrub, swamps, urban areas

The gregarious Chimney Swift is unrelated to the swallows but similar in shape. The body is like a fat torpedo with a very short tail and long, pointed, bowed wings that bend close to the body. It is dark brown overall and slightly paler underneath and at the chin. Constantly on the wing, it catches insects in flight with quick wing beats and fast glides. It never perches, but roosts at night on vertical cliffs, trees, or in chimneys. Its voice is a quick chattering uttered in flight. The illustration shows an adult.

Ruby-throated Hummingbird,
Archilochus colubris
Family Trochilidae (Hummingbirds)
Size: 3.5"
Season: Summer; year-round in southern Florida
Habitat: Areas with flowering plants, gardens, urban feeders

The Ruby-throated Hummingbird is a small, delicate bird able to hover on wings that beat at a blinding speed. The long, needle-like bill is used to probe deep into flowers so the bird can lap up the nectar. Its feet are tiny, and its body is white below and green above. Males have a dark green crown and iridescent red throat, or gorget. Females lack the colored gorget and have a light green crown and white-tipped tail feathers. Their behavior is typical of hummingbirds, hovering and buzzing from flower to flower, emitting chits and squeaks. Most of these birds migrate across the Gulf of Mexico to South America in the winter. The illustration shows an adult male, below, and female, above.

Belted Kingfisher,
Megaceryle alcyon
Family Alcedinidae (Kingfishers)
Size: 13″
Season: Year-round in Florida
Habitat: Creeks, lakes, sheltered coastline

The widespread but solitary Belted Kingfisher is a stocky, large-headed bird with a powerful, long bill and shaggy crest. It is gray-ish blue-green above and white below with a thick, blue band across the breast and white dotting on the back. At the lores is a white spot. The female has an extra breast band of rufous and rufous along the flanks. Belted Kingfishers feed by springing from a perch along the water's edge or hovering above the water, and then plunging headfirst to snatch fish, frogs, or tadpoles. Its flight is uneven and its voice is a raspy, rattling sound. The illustration shows an adult female.

Red-headed Woodpecker,
Melanerpes erythrocephalus
Family Picidae (Woodpeckers)
Size: 9″
Season: Year-round in central and northern Florida
Habitat: Woodlands, areas with standing dead trees, suburbs

The Red-headed Woodpecker has a striking bright red head and a powerful, tapered bill. It is black above with a large patch of white across the lower back and secondaries, and white below. The juvenile has a pale brown head and incomplete white back patch. In all woodpeckers the tail is very stiff, with sharp tips to aid in support while clinging to a tree trunk. To feed, it pecks at bark for insects but may also fly out to snatch its prey in midair. Nuts will also be taken and stored in tree cavities for winter. This species has been losing nesting cavities since the introduction of the European Starling. The illustration shows an adult.

Red-bellied Woodpecker,
Melanerpes carolinus
Family Picidae (Woodpeckers)
Size: 9"
Season: Year-round in Florida
Habitat: Woodlands, wooded swamps, parks, urban areas

The Red-bellied Woodpecker is a fairly common, large-billed woodpecker with extensively barred back and wings. The underparts are pale buff with a barely discernable hint of rose on the belly that gives the bird its name. The crown and nape are reddish-orange. Females lack the red crown, and juveniles have an entirely gray head. Like all woodpeckers, the Red-bellied Woodpecker has two toes pointing forward and two toes pointing back to allow a secure grip on tree trunks as it pecks away bark to find insects. It also feeds on nuts and oranges. Its flight is undulating wing beats and glides. The illustration shows an adult.

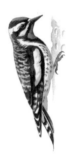

Yellow-bellied Sapsucker,
Sphyrapicus varius
Family Picidae (Woodpeckers)
Size: 8.5"
Season: Winter in Florida
Habitat: Woodlands, swamps, scrub

The sapsuckers are so named for their habit of drilling rows of pits in tree back, and then returning to eat the sap that emerges and the insects that come to investigate. They will also flycatch and eat berries. The Yellow-bellied Sapsucker is medium-size with pied black-and-white plumage and barring across the back. The head is boldly patterned black and white with a red crown and red chin (white in females). The belly is unbarred and pale yellow, while the surrounding flanks are white with black barring. In flight there is a distinct white patch on the upper wing. The illustration shows an adult male.

Downy Woodpecker,
Picoides pubescens
Family Picidae (Woodpeckers)
Size: 6.5"
Season: Year-round in Florida
Habitat: Woodlands, parks, urban areas, streamsides

The Downy Woodpecker is a tiny woodpecker with a small bill and relatively large head. It is white underneath with no barring, has black wings barred with white, and a patch of white on the back. The head is boldly patterned white and black, and the male sports a red nape patch. The base of the bill joins the head with fluffy nasal tufts. Juveniles may show some red on the forehead and crown. It forages for berries and insects in the bark and smaller twigs of trees. The very similar Hairy Woodpecker is larger with a longer bill and more aggressive foraging behavior, sticking to larger branches and not clinging to twigs. The illustration shows an adult male.

Red-cockaded Woodpecker,
Picoides borealis
Family Picidae (Woodpeckers)
Size: 8.5"
Season: Year-round in Florida
Habitat: Old-growth pine forests

The Red-cockaded Woodpecker nests only in mature pine trees, and is therefore rare and declining in numbers as it loses this habitat to development. It is a thin-looking, medium-size woodpecker with a long tail. Plumage is barred with black and white on the back and is white beneath with numerous spots and bars. The patterned head has a large white cheek patch and nasal tufts. The red cockade spot at the back of the crown on the male is rarely apparent in the field. Juveniles show a red forehead spot. This bird forms small groups called clans that forage together, pecking into tree bark for beetles and other insects. The illustration shows an adult male.

Northern Flicker, *Colaptes auratus*
Family Picidae (Woodpeckers)
Size: 12.5"
Season: Year-round in Florida
Habitat: A variety of habitats, including suburbs and parks

The common Northern Flicker is a large, long-tailed woodpecker often seen foraging on the ground for ants and other small insects. It is barred brown and black across the back, and buff below with black spotting. The head is brown with a gray nape and crown and a small red patch behind the head. On the upper breast is a prominent half-circle of black, and the male has a black patch at the malar region. Its flight is undulating and shows the golden yellow wing lining and white rump. Its voice is a loud, sharp *keee*, and it will sometimes drum its bill repeatedly at objects like a jack-hammer. The illustration shows an adult male.

Pileated Woodpecker, *Dryocopus pileatus*
Family Picidae (Woodpeckers)
Size: 16.5"
Season: Year-round in Florida
Habitat: Old-growth forests, urban areas with large trees

The Pileated Woodpecker is our largest woodpecker, except for the probably extinct, huge, Ivory-billed Woodpecker. It is very large, powerful, long-necked, and crested. The body is all black with a white base to the primaries which are mostly covered in the folded wing. The head is boldly patterned black and white with a bright red crest that is limited on the female. The male has a red malar patch instead of the black of the female. In flight one can see the contrasting white wing lining. To forage, Pileated Woodpeckers chip away chunks of bark to uncover ants and beetles, but will feed on berries during winter months. Its voice is a high-pitched, uneven, resounding *wok-wok-wok*. The illustration shows an adult male.

PASSERINES

Great Crested Flycatcher,
Myiarchus crinitus
Family Tyrannidae (Tyrant Flycatchers)
Size: 8.5"
Season: Year-round in southern Florida, summer in northern Florida
Habitat: Open woodlands and scrub, urban areas

The Great Crested Flycatcher is a large flycatcher with a proportionately large head and full crest. The upperparts and head are olive-brown, and the throat and breast are gray with a bright yellow belly. The primaries and tail show rufous color, while the margins to the tertials and coverts are white. Both sexes and the juvenile are similar in plumage. In flight note the yellow wing linings and rufous tail. It feeds by flying from perch to perch, catching insects in flight. It is often seen erecting its crown feathers and bobbing its head. Its voice is a high-pitched, whistling *wheeeerup!* The illustration shows an adult.

Gray Kingbird, *Tyrannus dominicensis*
Family Tyrannidae (Tyrant Flycatchers)
Size: 9"
Season: Summer in Florida
Habitat: Coastal regions of open woodland and scrub

Florida is the only state in which to reliably find this bird in the United States. The Gray Kingbird is a chunky, large-billed flycatcher with a fairly long tail. It is gray above and white below with a darker ear patch and lores, contrasting with the white lower half of the face. The bill is black, and the tail is notched at the tip. In flight the light underside of the wings is visible. Gray Kingbirds spring from their perches on posts, treetops, or wires and catch insects in flight. The illustration shows an adult.

Blue Jay, *Cyanocitta cristata*
Family Corvidae (Jays, Crows)
Size: 11"
Season: Year-round in Florida
Habitat: Woodlands, rural and urban areas

The solitary Blue Jay is a sturdy, crested jay. It is bright blue above and white below with a thick, tapered, black bill. There is a white patch around the eye to the chin, bordered by a thin, black "necklace" extending to the back of the nape. It has a conspicuous white wing bar and dark barring on wings and tail. In flight the white outer edges of the tail are visible as it alternates shallow wing beats with glides. Omnivorous, the Blue Jay eats just about anything, especially acorns, nuts, fruits, insects, and small vertebrates. It is a raucous and noisy bird and quite bold. Sometimes it mimics the calls of birds of prey. The illustration shows an adult.

Florida Scrub Jay,
Aphelocoma coerulescens
Family Corvidae (Jays, Crows)
Size: 11"
Season: Year-round in Florida
Habitat: Open scrub oak, urban areas

The Florida Scrub Jay is a rare bird, declining in numbers with the loss of habitat. It is a long-necked, sleek, crestless jay. Upperparts are deep blue with a distinct, lighter, gray-brown mantle. Underparts are pale gray, lightly streaked with brown. The forehead is white and the throat is streaked with white above a blue "necklace" across the breast. Its flight is an undulating combination of rapid wing beats and swooping glides. Its food consists of nuts, seeds, insects, and fruit. The illustration shows an adult.

American Crow,
Corvus brachyrhynchos
Family Corvidae (Jays, Crows)
Size: 17.5"
Season: Year-round in Florida
Habitat: Open woodlands, pastures, rural fields, dumps

The American Crow is a widespread corvid found across the continent voicing its familiar, loud, grating *caw, caw*. It is a large, stocky bird with a short, rounded tail, broad wings, and a thick, powerful bill. Plumage is overall glistening black in all stages. It will eat almost anything, often forming loose flocks with other crows. The illustration shows an adult.

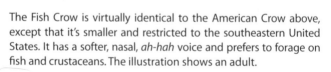

Fish Crow, *Corvus ossifragus*
Family Corvidae (Jays, Crows)
Size: 15"
Season: Year-round in Florida
Habitat: Coastal marshes, rivers, agricultural areas

The Fish Crow is virtually identical to the American Crow above, except that it's smaller and restricted to the southeastern United States. It has a softer, nasal, *ah-hah* voice and prefers to forage on fish and crustaceans. The illustration shows an adult.

Purple Martin, *Progne subis*
Family Hirundinidae (Swallows)
Size: 8"
Season: Summer in Florida
Habitat: Marshes, open water,
agricultural areas

The Purple Martin is the largest North American swallow. It has long, pointed wings, a streamlined body, and a forked tail. The bill is very short and broad at the base. The male is dark overall with a blackish-blue sheen across the back and head, while the female is paler overall with sooty, mottled underparts. Its flight consists of fast wing beats alternating with circular glides. Purple Martins commonly use man-made nest boxes or tree hollows to nest. The illustration shows an adult male.

SWALLOWS

Northern Rough-winged Swallow,
Stelgidopteryx serripennis
Family Hirundinidae (Swallows)
Size: 5.5"
Season: Year-round in southern Florida,
summer in northern Florida
Habitat: Sandy cliffs, riverbanks,
outcrops, bridges

The Northern Rough-winged Swallow flies in a smooth and even fashion with full wing beats, feeding on insects caught on the wing. It is uniformly brownish above and white below. The breast is lightly streaked with pale brown, and the tail is short and square. Juveniles show light, rust-colored wing bars on the upper coverts. These fairly solitary swallows find nesting sites in holes in sandy cliffs. The illustration shows an adult.

Tree Swallow, *Tachycineta bicolor*
Family Hirundinidae (Swallows)
Size: 5.75"
Season: Winter in Florida
Habitat: Variety of habitat near water
and perching sites

The Tree Swallow has a short, slightly notched tail, broad-based, triangular wings, and a thick neck. It has a high-contrast plumage pattern with dark metallic green-blue upperparts and crisp white underparts. In the perched bird, the primaries reach just past the tail tip. Juveniles show gray-brown below with a subtle, darker breast band. Tree Swallows take insects on the wing but will also eat berries and fruits. Their voice is a high-pitched chirping. They often form huge lines of individuals perched on wires or branches. The illustration shows an adult male.

Barn Swallow, *Hirundo rustica*
Family Hirundinidae (Swallows)
Size: 6.5"
Season: Summer in northern and central Florida, southern Florida during migration
Habitat: Open rural areas near bridges, old buildings, caves

The widespread and common Barn Swallow has narrow, pointed wings and a long, deeply forked tail. It is pale below and dark blue above with a rusty orange forehead and throat. In males the underparts are pale orange, while females are pale cream below. Barn Swallows are graceful, fluid fliers, and they often forage in groups while catching insects in flight. Their voice is a loud, repetitive chirping or clicking. They build a cup-shaped nest of mud on almost any protected man-made structure. The illustration shows an adult male.

Tufted Titmouse,

Baeolophus bicolor
Family Paridae (Chickadees, Titmice)
Size: 6.5"
Season: Year-round in Florida
Habitat: Woodlands, urban areas

The tame and curious Tufted Titmouse is a small, chunky bird with short, broad wings and a conspicuous tuft on the crest. It is gray above and pale gray below with a wash of orange along the sides and flanks. It has a small but sturdy black bill, large black eyes, and a black forehead. It often forms foraging groups with other species that flit through the vegetation picking out nuts, seeds, insects, and berries from the bark and twigs. At feeders, the Tufted Titmouse prefers sunflower seeds. Its voice is a repetitive *peeta peeta*. The illustration shows an adult.

CHICKADEES, TITMICE

Carolina Chickadee,

Poecile carolinensis
Family Paridae (Chickadees, Titmice)
Size: 4.75"
Season: Year-round in northern and central Florida
Habitat: Woodland areas, feeders

The Carolina Chickadee is a small, compact, active bird with short, rounded wings. It is gray above and lighter gray or dusky below with a contrasting black cap and throat patch. It is quite similar to the Black-capped Chickadee, which does not normally occur in Florida. Its voice sounds like the name, *chick-a-dee, dee, dee*, or a soft *fee-bay*. It is quite social and feeds on a variety of seeds, berries, and insects found in trees and shrubs. The illustration shows an adult.

Brown-headed Nuthatch,
Sitta pusilla
Family Sittidae (Nuthatches)
Size: 4.5"
Season: Year-round in Florida
Habitat: Pine woodlands

Clinging to tree trunks facing downward, the little Brown-headed Nuthatch creeps its way down the tree picking out insects, larvae, or seeds from the bark. It is a compact, short-necked, large-headed bird with a short, stubby tail. Legs are short, but toes are long to help grasp bark. The bill is long, thin, sharp, and upturned at the tip. Plumage is gray above and lighter gray or buffy below. On the head are a brown cap, a dark eye line, and a small white spot on the back of the nape. They have undulating flight and nest in cavities in the tree trunks. The illustration shows an adult.

Carolina Wren,
Thryothorus ludovicianus
Family Troglodytidae (Wrens)
Size: 5.5"
Season: Year-round in Florida
Habitat: Understory of wooded and brushy areas, swamps

The Carolina Wren is a vocal but cryptic bird, usually hidden among dense foliage close to the ground. It lurks in vegetation picking out insects, seeds, or fruit, emitting a musical song or a harsh, quick call. The body is plump with a short, rounded tail and a thin, slightly down-curved bill. It is dark rusty-brown above, buffy below, and has a long, white superciliary stripe extending to the nape. Wings and tail are thinly barred with black. This bird habitually holds its tail in a cocked-up position. The illustration shows an adult.

Winter Wren,
Troglodytes hiemalis
Family Troglodytidae (Wrens)
Size: 4"
Season: Winter in Florida (Panhandle region)
Habitat: Moist woodlands, streams

The Winter Wren is a tiny, short-tailed, and plump wren that is brown overall with dark mottling and barring. It is a bit paler on the throat and breast and has a distinct pale supercilium. The tail is commonly held cocked up and the bill is held slightly tilted up. It forages through dense vegetation searching for insects. Inquisitive and curious, Winter Wrens may be lured into view by imitating their high-pitched, buzzy calls. The illustration shows an adult.

Marsh Wren, *Cistothorus palustris*
Family Troglodytidae (Wrens)
Size: 5"
Season: Year-round in Florida
Habitat: Marshes, reeds, stream banks

The Marsh Wren is a small, cryptic, rufous-brown wren with a normally cocked-up tail. The tail and wings are barred with black, and the chin and breast are white. There is a well-defined white superciliary stripe below a uniform brown crown, and the mantle shows distinct black-and-white striping. The bill is long and slightly decurved. Marsh Wrens are vocal day and night with quick, repetitive, cheeping. They are secretive but inquisitive, and glean insects from the marsh vegetation and water surface. The illustration shows an adult.

Blue-gray Gnatcatcher,
Polioptila caerulea
Family Polioptilidae (Gnatcatchers)
Size: 4.5"
Season: Year-round in Florida
Habitat: Deciduous or pine woodlands, thickets

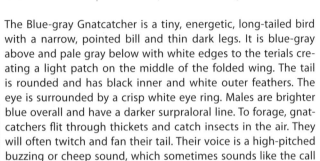

The Blue-gray Gnatcatcher is a tiny, energetic, long-tailed bird with a narrow, pointed bill and thin dark legs. It is blue-gray above and pale gray below with white edges to the terials creating a light patch on the middle of the folded wing. The tail is rounded and has black inner and white outer feathers. The eye is surrounded by a crisp white eye ring. Males are brighter blue overall and have a darker surpraloral line. To forage, gnatcatchers flit through thickets and catch insects in the air. They will often twitch and fan their tail. Their voice is a high-pitched buzzing or cheep sound, which sometimes sounds like the call of other birds. The illustration shows an adult male.

Red-whiskered Bulbul,
Pycnonotus jocosus
Family Pycnonotidae (Bulbuls)
Size: 7"
Season: Year-round in the southern tip of Florida
Habitat: Suburban gardens, parks with shrubs, agricultural areas

Introduced from Asia, the Red-whiskered Bulbul is a stocky bird with a long tail, an obvious pointed crest tuft, and a boldly patterned face. It is brown above and white below with light brown sides and flanks. A dark arc crosses the breast and a thin dark stripe borders the lower face. Bright red "whiskers" emerge from behind the eye, and the undertail coverts are bright orange-red. Its flight is uneven with short, rounded wings. It forages on berries, fruit, and small insects. The illustration shows an adult.

Ruby-crowned Kinglet,
Regulus calendula
Family Regulidae (Kinglets)
Size: 4"
Season: Winter in Florida
Habitat: Mixed woodlands, shrubbery

The Ruby-crowned Kinglet is a tiny, plump songbird with a short tail and diminutive, thin bill. It has a habit of nervously twitching its wings as it actively flits through vegetation gleaning small insects and larvae. It may also hover in search of food. Plumage is pale olive-green above, paler below, with patterned wings of pale wingbars on the upper coverts. There are white eye rings or crescents around the eyes. The bright red crest of the male bird is faintly noticeable unless the crest is raised. Its voice is a very high-pitched, whistling *seeee*. The illustration shows an adult.

Eastern Bluebird, *Sialia sialis*
Family Turdidae (Thrushes)
Size: 7"
Season: Year-round in Florida
Habitat: Open woodland, pastures, fields

The Eastern Bluebird is a member of the thrush family that travels in small groups, feeding on a variey of insects, spiders, and berries and singing a series of musical *chur-lee* notes. It is a stocky, short-tailed and short-billed bird that often perches in an upright posture on wires and posts. The male is brilliant blue above and rusty-orange below with a white belly and undertail region. The orange extends to the nape making a subtle collar. The female is paler overall with a white throat and eye ring. Juveniles are brownish-gray with extensive white spotting and barred underparts. Man-made nest boxes have helped this species increase in numbers throughout its range. The illustration shows an adult male, below, and female, above.

American Robin,
Turdus migratorius
Family Turdidae (Thrushes)
Size: 10"
Season: Winter in Florida
Habitat: Widespread in a variety of habitats; woodlands, fields, parks, lawns

Familiar and friendly, the American Robin is a large thrush with a long tail and legs. It commonly holds its head cocked and wing tips lowered beneath its tail. It is gray-brown above and rufous below with a darker head and contrasting white eye crescents and loral patch. The chin is streaked black and white and the bill is yellow mixed with darker edges. Females are typically paler overall, and the juvenile shows spotting of white above and dark below. Robins forage on the ground, picking out earthworms and insects, or in trees to find berries. Their song is a series of high, musical phrases like *cheery, cheeruup, cheerio*. The illustration shows an adult male.

THRUSHES

Hermit Thrush, *Catharus guttatus*
Family Turdidae (Thrushes)
Size: 7"
Season: Winter in Florida
Habitat: Woodlands, brushy areas

The Hermit Thrush is a compact, short-tailed thrush that habitually cocks its tail. It forages on the ground near vegetative cover for insects, worms, and berries and voices its song of beautiful, flutelike notes. It is reddish to olive brown above with a rufous tail. Underparts are white with dusky flanks and sides and black spotting on the throat and breast. The dark eyes are encircled by a complete, white eye ring. In flight the pale wing lining contrasts with the dark flight feathers. The illustration shows an adult.

Gray Catbird, *Dumetella carolinensis*

Family Mimidae (Mockingbirds, Catbirds, Thrashers)
Size: 8.5"
Season: Year-round in northern Florida,
winter elsewhere
Habitat: Understory of woodland edges,
shrubs, rural gardens

The solitary Gray Catbird is long-necked and sleek with a sturdy, pointed bill. It is uniformly gray except for its rufous undertail coverts, black crown, and black, rounded tail. It is quite secretive and spends most of its time hidden in thickets close to the ground, picking through the substrate for insects, berries, and seeds. Its call includes a nasal, catlike *meew* from which its name is derived, although it will also mimic the songs of other birds. To escape danger, it will often choose to run away rather than fly. The illustration shows an adult.

Northern Mockingbird,
Mimus polyglottos
Family Mimidae (Mockingbirds, Catbirds, Thrashers)
Size: 10.5"
Season: Year-round in Florida
Habitat: Open fields, grassy areas near
vegetative cover, suburbs, parks

The Northern Mockingbird is the state bird of Florida. It is constantly vocalizing, and its scientific name, *polyglottos*, means "many voices," alluding to its amazing mimicry of the songs of other birds. It is sleek, long-tailed, and long-legged. Plumage is gray above with darker wings and tail and off-white to brownish-gray below. There are two white wing bars, a short, dark eye stripe, and a pale eye ring. In flight note the conspicuous white patch on the inner primaries and coverts, and white outer tail feathers. Like other mimids, it forages on the ground for insects and berries, intermittently flicking its wings. The illustration shows an adult.

Brown Thrasher,
Toxostoma rufum
Family Mimidae (Mockingbirds, Catbirds, Thrashers)
Size: 11"
Season: Year-round in Florida
Habitat: Woodlands, thickets, urban gardens, orchards

The Brown Thrasher is primarily a ground-dwelling bird that thrashes through leaves and dirt for insects and plant material. It has a long tail and legs with a medium length, slightly decurved bill. Plumage is rufous-brown above, including the tail, and whitish below, heavily streaked with brown or black. There are two prominent, pale wing bars and pale outermost corners to the tail. Its eye is yellow to orange. Its voice is a variety of musical phrases, often sung from a conspicuous perch. The illustration shows an adult.

European Starling, *Sturnus vulgaris*
Family Sturnidae (Starlings)
Size: 8.5"
Season: Year-round in Florida
Habitat: Found almost anywhere, particularly rural fields, gardens, dumps, urban parks

Introduced from Europe, the European Starling has successfully infiltrated most habitats in North America and competes with native birds for nest cavities. It is a stocky, sturdy, and aggressive bird that is overall glossy black with a sheen of green or purple. The breeding adult has a yellow bill and greater iridescence, while the winter adult is colored a more flat black with a black bill and numerous white spots. Its tail is short and square. European Starlings form very large, compact flocks and fly directly on pointed, triangular wings. Their diet is highly variable and includes insects, grains, and berries. Their voice consists of loud, wheezy, whistles and clucks and imitations of other bird songs. The illustration shows a breeding adult.

Cedar Waxwing,
Bombycilla cedrorum
Family Bombycillidae (Waxwings)
Size: 7"
Season: Winter in Florida
Habitat: Woodlands, swamps, urban areas near berry trees

The Cedar Waxwing is a compact, crested songbird with pointed wings and a short tail. Plumage is sleek and smooth, overall brownish-gray with paler underparts, a yellowish wash on the belly, and white undertail coverts. The head pattern is striking with a crisp black mask thinly bordered by white. The tail is tipped with bright yellow. Tips of the secondary feathers are a unique, red, waxy substance. Cedar Waxwings will form large flocks and devour berries from one tree, and then move on to the next. They may also flycatch for small insects. Their voice is an extremely high-pitched, whistling *see*. The illustration shows an adult.

Northern Parula,
Parula americana
Family Parulidae (Wood-Warblers)
Size: 4.5"
Season: Year-round in Florida
Habitat: Treetops in mossy woodlands

The Northern Parula is a tiny, stubby warbler with a short, sharp bill, short tail, and a relatively large head. Upperparts are slatey blue with a greenish mantle. Below there is a white belly and undertail, a yellow chin and breast, and a rufous breast band. Above and below the eyes are white eye arcs, and the lower mandible is yellow. The wing shows two bold white wing bars. The female is bordered above the breast band with gray. Northern Parulas forage for insects and caterpillars in trees. The illustration shows an adult male.

Yellow Warbler,
Dendroica petechia
Family Parulidae (Wood-Warblers)
Size: 5"
Season: Year-round in the southern tip of Florida
Habitat: Willows and alders near streamsides, rural shrubbery, gardens

The Yellow Warbler is a widespread warbler of North America with a musical voice of *sweet-sweet-sweet*. It is overall bright yellow with darker yellow-green above and reddish-brown streaking below. The black eyes stand out on its light face, and the bill is relatively thick for a warbler. Clean, yellow stripes are evident on the fanned tail. The female is paler overall with less noticeable streaking on the breast and sides. They forage among the brush for insects and spiders. The illustration shows an adult male.

Yellow-rumped Warbler (Myrtle Warbler),
Dendroica coronata coronata
Family Parulidae (Wood-Warblers)
Size: 5.5"
Season: Winter in Florida
Habitat: Deciduous and coniferous woodlands, suburbs with wax myrtle

Two races of this species occur in North America. In Florida we have the "Myrtle" form, and east of the Rockies there is the "Audubon's" form. The Myrtle Warbler is blue-gray above with dark streaks, and white below with black streaking below the chin and a bright yellow side patch. There is a black mask across the face bordered by a thin superciliary stripe above and white throat below. The nonbreeding adult and female are paler with a more brownish cast to the upperparts. The longish tail has white spots on either side and meets with the conspicuous yellow rump. It prefers to eat myrtle berries and insects. The illustration shows a "Myrtle" breeding male.

Prairie Warbler,

Dendroica discolor
Family Parulidae (Wood-Warblers)
Size: 4.5"
Season: Year-round in Florida
Habitat: Mangroves, early succession forests, shrubs

The Prairie Warbler is a small, plump, long-tailed warbler with a rising, buzzy song, sometimes sung from a treetop perch. It is olive-green above and bright yellow below with black streaking along its sides topped by a distinct spot just behind the bottom of the chin. A dark half-circle swoops underneath the eye, and sometimes rusty streaking is seen on the mantle. The female is slightly paler overall. The outer tail feathers are white. Prairie Warblers forage through low branches of the understory for insects and spiders. The illustration shows an adult male.

Palm Warbler,

Dendroica palmarum
Family Parulidae (Wood-Warblers)
Size: 5.5"
Season: Winter in Florida
Habitat: Thickets near spruce bogs, open grassland

The Palm Warbler forages on the ground for insects while constantly bobbing its tail. It is brownish above with darker streaking, and pale brown-gray below with dark streaking. Chin and undertail coverts are bright yellow. The head has a dark eye stripe, a pale superciliary stripe, and a dark, rufous crown. Nonbreeding adults are paler with a gray chin and brown crown. Outer tail feathers show small white patches and contrast with an olive-yellow rump. Two races of this species occur in Florida: the "yellow" with a yellow underside, and the "brown" with a pale gray belly and brown streaking. The illustration shows a breeding adult, "brown" form.

Pine Warbler, *Dendroica pinus*
Family Parulidae (Wood-Warblers)
Size: 5.5"
Season: Year-round in central and northern Florida
Habitat: Pine and mixed-pine woodlands

The Pine Warbler creeps along pine branches picking insects from the bark. It is a rounded, long-winged warbler with a relatively thick bill. Plumage is olive-green above with gray wings, and yellow below streaked with olive. Belly and undertail coverts are white. The yellow of the chin extends under the auricular area; a faint "spectacle" is formed by the light lores and eye ring, and there are two clearly marked white wing bars. The female is paler overall, and the juvenile lacks yellow on the chin and underparts. The outer tail feathers show white patches. The illustration shows an adult male.

Yellow-throated Warbler, *Dendroica dominica*
Family Parulidae (Wood-Warblers)
Size: 5.25"
Season: Year-round in Florida
Habitat: Coniferous and mixed woodlands near water

The Yellow-throated Warbler is an elongated, long-billed warbler that forages high in the tree canopy picking insects from the bark. Its plumage is slate-gray above and white below, heavily streaked with black, and it has a clean yellow chin and breast. There is a bold face pattern with a white supercilium and lower eye arc bordered by a black eye stripe and auricular area. Behind the ear is a distinctive white patch. The dark back contrasts with two white wing bars. The outer tail feathers show patches of white. The illustration shows an adult male.

WOOD-WARBLERS

Prothonotary Warbler,
Protonotaria citrea
Family Parulidae (Wood-Warblers)
Size: 5.5"
Season: Summer in Florida
Habitat: Wooded swamps

Also known as the Golden Swamp Warbler, the Prothonotary Warbler is a fairly large warbler with a short tail, a relatively large head, and a long, sharp bill. The head and underparts are a rich yellow to yellow-orange, and the undertail coverts are white. The wings and tail are blue-gray and there is an olive-green mantle. Females and juveniles are paler overall with an olive cast to the head. Prothonotary Warblers forage through the understory for insects. The illustration shows an adult male.

American Redstart,
Setophaga ruticilla
Family Parulidae (Wood-Warblers)
Size: 5"
Season: Summer in Florida
Habitat: Open mixed woodlands in early succession

The constantly active, frenetic American Redstart often fans its tail and wings in display while perched. It is long-tailed, and the plumages of males and females are markedly different. The male is jet black above, white below, with a fiery red patch at the side of the breast, and a paler, peachy-red wing bar and sides of the tail. The female is gray-green above with a slatey-gray head and white chin and breast. The colored areas are located in the same areas of the male but are yellow. Redstarts eat insects gleaned from branches and bark, or they flycatch for insects. The illustration shows an adult male, below, and female, above.

Common Yellowthroat,
Geothlypis trichas
Family Parulidae (Wood-Warblers)
Size: 5″
Season: Year-round in Florida
Habitat: Low vegetation near water, swamps, fields

The Common Yellowthroat scampers through the undergrowth for insects and spiders in a somewhat wrenlike manner. It is a plump little warbler that often cocks up its tail. Plumage is olive-brown above, pale brown to whitish below, with bright yellow undertail coverts and breast/chin region. The male has a black facial mask trailed by a fuzzy white area on the nape. Females lack the facial mask. The illustration shows an adult male, below, and female, above.

Hooded Warbler,
Wilsonia citrina
Family Parulidae (Wood-Warblers)
Size: 5″
Season: Year-round except midwinter in Florida
Habitat: Moist woodlands, swamps

The Hooded Warbler lurks in the woodland understory picking out insects while continually flicking its tail and singing its high, musical *weeta-weeta-weeta-toe*. Plumage is olive-green above and bright yellow below. The male has a full, black hood encompassing the face and chin, while the female has a fainter, partial mask with a yellow chin. In the fanned tail one can see white inner vanes to the outer tail feathers. The illustration shows an adult male, below, and female, above.

Eastern Towhee,

Pipilo erythrophthalmus
Family Emberizidae (Sparrows)
Size: 8″
Season: Year-round in Florida
Habitat: Thickets, suburban shrubs, gardens

The Eastern Towhee is a large, long-tailed sparrow with a thick, short bill and sturdy legs. It forages on the ground in dense cover by kicking back both feet at once to uncover insects, seeds, and worms. It is black above, including the head and upper breast, and it has rufous sides and a white belly. The base of the primaries is white as are the corners of the tail. Eye color ranges from red to white, depending on the region. Females are like the males but brown above. Its song is a musical *drink-your-teee*. The Eastern Towhee was once conspecific with the Spotted Towhee as the Rufous-sided Towhee. The illustration shows an adult male.

Chipping Sparrow,

Spizella passerina
Family Emberizidae (Sparrows)
Size: 5.5″
Season: Year-round in Florida
Habitat: Dry fields, woodland edges, gardens

The Chipping Sparrow is a medium-size sparrow with a slightly notched tail and a rounded crest. It is barred black and brown on the upperparts with a gray rump and is pale gray below. On the head are a rufous crown, a white superciliary stripe, a dark eye line, and a white throat. The bill is short, conical, and pointed. Sexes are similar, and winter adults are duller and lack rufous on the crown. Chipping Sparrows feed from trees or open ground in loose flocks, searching for seeds and insects. Their voice is a rapid, staccato chipping sound. The illustration shows a breeding adult.

Saltmarsh Sparrow,

Ammodramus caudacutus
Family Emberizidae (Sparrows)
Size: 5.25"
Season: Winter in Florida
Habitat: Salt- or freshwater marshes, grasslands

The Saltmarsh Sparrow is a ground-dwelling, thick-necked sparrow with a flatish crown. Its tail is short with pointed feathers, which is how it gets its name. Plumage is streaked brownish above with contrasting white streaks, while the underside is white, heavily streaked, with an orange wash on the sides. The nape is gray, and the crown and auriculars are dark, surrounded by an orange superciliary stripe, ear patch, and malar area. This bird stays low to the ground, even in flight, and quickly dives for cover. It was once considered conspecific with the Nelson's Sparrow, as the Sharp-tailed Sparrow. The illustration shows an adult.

Seaside Sparrow (Cape Sable ssp.),

Ammodramus maritimus mirabilis
Family Emberizidae (Sparrows)
Size: 6"
Season: Year-round in Florida
Habitat: Coastal saltwater marshes, freshwater marshes

One of several similar races of this species, the Cape Sable Seaside Sparrow breeds in southern Florida. It is plump with a relatively large, flat head, a fairly long bill, and a short tail. Plumage is olive-brown above with dark streaking, and white below with dark streaks or spots. The chin is white, bordered by an obvious moustachial stripe, and the supraloral region is yellow. This bird forages among the marsh vegetation for insects, seeds, and small crustaceans and snails. It dives quickly into cover from flight. The illustration shows an adult.

White-thoated Sparrow,
Zonotrichia albicollis
Family Emberizidae (Sparrows)
Size: 6.5"
Season: Winter in Florida
Habitat: Undergrowth of mixed woodlands, thickets, gardens

The White-throated Sparrow is a fairly large, rounded sparrow with a long tail and typical short, thick bill. It is brown with dark streaking above, has a gray rump, and is grayish below, washed with brown and lightly streaked. The head has a black crown that is bisected by a white medial strip, a white superciliary stripe with yellow near the lores, and a dark eye line. The white chin is sharply bordered by the gray breast below. White-throated Sparrows forage on the ground in small flocks, often with other species, picking up insects and seeds. Their song is a clean, piercing, simple whistle that mimics the phrase, *old sam peabody, peabody, peabody*. The illustration shows an adult.

Song Sparrow, *Melospiza melodia*
Family Emberizidae (Sparrows)
Size: 6"
Season: Winter in Florida
Habitat: Thickets, shrubs, woodland edges near water

One of our most common sparrows, the Song Sparrow is fairly plump with a long, rounded tail. It is brown and gray with streaking above, and white below with heavy dark streaking that often converges into a discreet spot in the middle of the breast. The head has a dark crown with a gray medial stripe, a dark eye line, and a dark malar stripe above the white chin. Song sparrows are usually seen in small groups or individually foraging on the ground for insects and seeds. Their call is a *chip, chip, chip,* which is more commonly heard than its song during winter. The illustration shows an adult.

Summer Tanager,
Piranga rubra
Family Cardinalidae (Cardinals, Tanagers, Grosbeaks, Buntings)
Size: 7.75″
Season: Summer in Florida, year-round in southern Florida
Habitat: Mixed pine and oak woodlands

The Summer Tanager lives high in the tree canopy, where it voices a musical song and forages for insects and fruit. It is a relatively large, heavy-billed tanager with a crown that is often peaked in the middle. The male is variable shades of red over the entire body, while the female is olive or brownish-yellow above and dull yellow below. Juveniles are similar to the females but have a patchy red head and breast. The illustration shows an adult male.

Northern Cardinal,
Cardinalis cardinalis
Family Cardinalidae (Cardinals, Tanagers, Grosbeaks, Buntings)
Size: 8.5″
Season: Year-round in Florida
Habitat: Woodlands with thickets, suburban gardens

The Northern Cardinal with its thick, powerful bill eats mostly seeds but will also forage for fruit and insects. It is often found in pairs and is quite common at suburban feeders. It is a long-tailed songbird with a thick, short, orange bill and a tall crest. The male is red overall with a black mask and chin. The female is brownish above, dusky below, crested, with a dark front to the face. Juveniles are similar to the female but have a black bill. The voice is a musical *weeta-weeta* or *woit* heard from a tall, exposed perch. The illustration shows an adult male, below, and female, above.

Blue Grosbeak,
Guiraca caerulea or *Passerina caerulea*
Family Cardinalidae (Cardinals, Tanagers,
Grosbeaks, Buntings)
Size: 6.5"
Season: Summer in Florida
Habitat: Woodland edges, thickets, fields

Grosbeaks are named from the French word, *gros,* meaning large, which refers to their massive, conical bills. The male Blue Grosbeak is azure blue overall with a rufous wing bar and shoulder patch, black at the front of the face with a horn-colored bill. The female is brown overall, and paler below with lighter wing bars and lores. The similar Indigo Bunting is smaller, smaller-billed, and lacks the rufous color on the wings. Blue Grosbeaks eat seeds, fruit, and insects in open areas, and habitually flick their tails. They often perch and sing for extended periods with a meandering, warbling song. The illustration shows an adult male, below, and female, above.

Indigo Bunting,
Passerina cyanea
Family Cardinalidae (Cardinals, Tanagers,
Grosbeaks, Buntings)
Size: 5.5"
Season: Summer in Florida
Habitat: Brush, open woodlands, fields

Often occurring in large flocks, the Indigo Bunting forages mostly on the ground for insects, berries, and seeds. It is a compact, small songbird with a short, thick bill. The male is entirely blue; the head is a dark, purplish-blue and the body is a lighter, sky blue. The female is brownish-gray above, duller below, with faint streaking on the breast meeting a white throat. The winter male is smudged with patchy gray, brown, and white. They perch in treetops voicing their undulating, chirping melodies. The illustration shows a breeding male, below, and female, above.

Painted Bunting, *Passerina ciris*
Family Cardinalidae (Cardinals, Tanagers, Grosbeaks, Buntings)
Size: 5.5"
Season: Winter in Florida
Habitat: Edges of woodlands, brushy areas, gardens

Like a rainbow on wings, the Painted Bunting is one of our most colorful birds. It is similar in shape to other buntings, and the plumage is markedly different between the sexes. The male has a green mantle and wings, red-orange to rusty underparts and rump, and a brilliant blue head with a red eye ring. The female is yellowish-green above and pale yellow-green below with a pale eye ring. Often secretive and difficult to find, Painted Buntings scamper in the low understory or on the ground for insects, seeds, and fruit. However, they may also visit feeders. The illustration shows an adult male, below, and female, above.

Eastern Meadowlark,
Sturnella magna
Family Icteridae (Blackbirds, Grackles, Orioles)
Size: 9.5"
Season: Year-round in Florida
Habitat: Open fields, grasslands, meadows

The Eastern Meadowlark is a chunky, short-tailed icterid with a flat head and a long, pointed bill. It is heavily streaked and barred above, and yellow beneath with dark streaking. The head has a dark crown, a white superciliary stripe, a dark eye line, and a yellow chin. On the upper breast is a black, V-shaped necklace that becomes quite pale during winter months. Meadowlarks gather in loose flocks to pick through the grass for insects and seeds. They often perch on telephone wires or posts to sing their short, whistling phrases. The illustration shows a breeding adult.

Bobolink, *Dolichonyx oryzivorus*
Family Icteridae (Blackbirds, Grackles, Orioles)
Size: 7"
Season: Spring and fall during migration through Florida
Habitat: Lush prairies, grassland, agricultural areas

Florida is a stopover region for the Bobolink, which migrates from the northern United States to South America. It is shaped like an elongated sparrow with pointy wings and exhibits quite different plumage between males and females. The female and winter male are buffy brown overall, paler below, with streaking along the back and sides. On the face is a thin, dark crown and eye stripe. The breeding male is white above and black below with a two-toned head that is black in front and light yellow in back. The voice is a playful, jumbled melody that some compare to its name, *bobolink-bobolink*. The illustration shows a breeding male, below, and female, above.

Brown-headed Cowbird, *Molothrus ater*
Family Icteridae (Blackbirds, Grackles, Orioles)
Size: 7.5"
Season: Year-round in Florida
Habitat: Woodland edges, pastures with livestock, grassy fields

The Brown-headed Cowbird is a stocky, short-winged, and short-tailed blackbird with a short, conical bill. The male is glossy black overall with a chocolate-brown head. The female is light brown overall with faint streaking on the underparts and a pale throat. They often feed in flocks with other blackbirds, picking out seeds and insects from the ground. The voice is a number of gurgling, squeaking phrases. Cowbirds practice brood parasitism, whereby they lay their eggs in the nests of other passerine species that then raise their young. Hence, their presence often reduces the populations of other songbirds. The illustration shows an adult male.

Red-winged Blackbird,
Agelaius phoeniceus
Family Icteridae (Blackbirds, Grackles, Orioles)
Size: 8.5"
Season: Year-round in Florida
Habitat: Marshes, meadows,
agricultural areas near water

The Red-winged Blackbird is a widespread, ubiquitous, chunky, meadow-dweller that will form huge flocks during the non-breeding season. The male is deep black overall with bright orange-red lesser coverts and pale median coverts that form an obvious shoulder patch in flight but may be partially concealed on the perched bird. The female is barred tan and dark brown overall with a pale superciliary stripe and malar patch. They forage the marshland for insects, spiders, and seeds. The voice is a loud, raspy, vibrating *konk-a-leee* given from a perch atop a tall reed or branch. The illustration shows an adult male, below, and female, above.

Common Grackle,
Quiscalus quiscula
Family Icteridae (Blackbirds, Grackles, Orioles)
Size: 12.5"
Season: Year-round in Florida
Habitat: Pastures, open woodlands, urban parks

The Common Grackle is a large blackbird but smaller than the Boat-tailed Grackle. The body is elongated with a long, heavy bill and long tail, which is fatter toward the tip and is often folded into a keel shape. Plumage is overall black with a metallic sheen of purple on the head and brown on the wings and underside. The eyes are a contrasting light yellow color. Quite social, Grackles form huge flocks with other blackbirds and forage on the ground for just about any kind of food, including insects, grains, refuse, and crustaceans. The voice is a high-pitched, rasping trill. The illustration shows an adult male.

Boat-tailed Grackle,
Quiscalus major
Family Icteridae (Blackbirds, Grackles, Orioles)
Size: 14–16"; males larger than females
Season: Year-round in Florida
Habitat: Salt- or freshwater marshes, pastures, urban parks

The Boat-tailed Grackle is larger than the Common Grackle and less likely to form large flocks. It has long legs and a long, broad, spatula-shaped tail that is often folded in a keel shape. The male is black overall with a metallic, blue-green sheen over the head and body. The female is smaller with a shorter tail, is brownish overall, and has a lighter head with dark striping along the eye line, under the crown, and along the malar area. The eyes of northern birds are light yellow, while those in southern Florida have darker, brown eyes. They pick the ground for insects, seeds, and crustaceans. The illustration shows an adult male, below, and a female, above.

Baltimore Oriole, *Icterus galbula*
Family Icteridae (Blackbirds, Grackles, Orioles)
Size: 8.5"
Season: Winter in Florida
Habitat: Deciduous woodlands, suburban gardens, parks

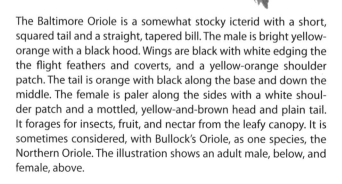

The Baltimore Oriole is a somewhat stocky icterid with a short, squared tail and a straight, tapered bill. The male is bright yellow-orange with a black hood. Wings are black with white edging the the flight feathers and coverts, and a yellow-orange shoulder patch. The tail is orange with black along the base and down the middle. The female is paler along the sides with a white shoulder patch and a mottled, yellow-and-brown head and plain tail. It forages for insects, fruit, and nectar from the leafy canopy. It is sometimes considered, with Bullock's Oriole, as one species, the Northern Oriole. The illustration shows an adult male, below, and female, above.

Orchard Oriole,
Icterus spurius
Family Icteridae (Blackbirds, Grackles, Orioles)
Size: 7"
Season: Summer in Florida
Habitat: Orchards, open woodlands, parks

The Orchard Oriole is a small oriole with a relatively thin, short bill, and a short tail that it often tilts sideways. The male is black above with a red rump and a black, hooded head. The underside is reddish or orange-brown with a similarly colored shoulder patch. The lower mandible is light, blue-gray. Females are markedly different, being greenish-gray above and bright yellow below with two white wing bars. The juvenile is similar to the female but has a black chin and lores. Orchard Orioles feed in trees for insects, fruit, and nectar, and emit high, erratic, musical whistles and chirps. The illustration shows an adult male, below, and female, above.

Spot-breasted Oriole,
Icterus pectoralis
Family Icteridae (Blackbirds, Grackles, Orioles)
Size: 9"
Season: Year-round in southeastern Florida
Habitat: Woodland edges, urban gardens

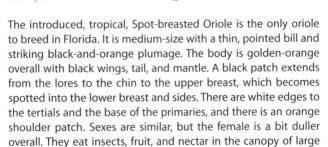

The introduced, tropical, Spot-breasted Oriole is the only oriole to breed in Florida. It is medium-size with a thin, pointed bill and striking black-and-orange plumage. The body is golden-orange overall with black wings, tail, and mantle. A black patch extends from the lores to the chin to the upper breast, which becomes spotted into the lower breast and sides. There are white edges to the tertials and the base of the primaries, and there is an orange shoulder patch. Sexes are similar, but the female is a bit duller overall. They eat insects, fruit, and nectar in the canopy of large trees. The illustration shows an adult.

90

House Finch, *Carpodacus mexicanus*
Family Fringillidae (Finches)
Size: 6"
Season: Year-round in the northern half of Florida
Habitat: Woodland edges, urban areas

The House Finch is a western species that has been introduced to eastern North America and is now common and widespread here, especially in urban areas. It is a relatively slim finch with a longish, slightly notched tail and a short, conical bill with a down-curved culmen. The male is brown above with streaking on the back, and pale below with heavy streaking. An orange-red wash pervades the supercilium, throat, and upper breast. The female is a drab gray-brown with similar streaking on the back and underside and no red on the face or breast. House Finches have a variable diet that includes seeds, insects, and fruit, and they are often the most abundant bird visiting feeders. The voice is a rapid, musical warble. The illustration shows an adult male.

American Goldfinch,
Spinus tristis
Family Fringillidae (Finches)
Size: 5"
Season: Winter in Florida
Habitat: Open fields, marshes, urban feeders

The American Goldfinch is a small, cheerful, social finch with a short, notched tail and a small, conical bill. In winter it is brownish-gray, lighter underneath, with black wings and tail. There is bright yellow on the shoulder, around the eyes, and along the chin, and there are two white wing bars. In breeding plumage, the male becomes light yellow across the back, undersides, and head and develops a black forehead and loral area. Also, the bill becomes orange. Females are similar to the winter males. They forage by actively searching for insects and seeds of all kinds, particularly thistle. Their voice is a meandering, musical warble, including high cheep notes. The illustration shows a breeding male, below, and a nonbreeding male, above.

House Sparrow, *Passer domesticus*
Family Passeridae (Old World Sparrows)
Size: 6.25"
Season: Year-round across North America
Habitat: Urban environments,
rural pastures

Introduced from Europe, the House Sparrow is ubiquitous in almost every city in the United States and is often the only sparrow-type bird seen in urban areas. It is stocky, aggressive, and gregarious, and has a relatively large head and a short, finchlike bill. Males are streaked brown and black above, and pale below. The lores, chin, and breast are black, while the crown and auriculars are gray. There is a prominent white wing bar at the median coverts. In winter the male lacks the dark breast patch. Females are drab overall with a lighter bill and a pale supercilium. House Sparrows have a highly varied diet, including grains, insects, berries, and crumbs from the local cafe. Their voice is a series of rather unmusical chirps. The illustration shows a breeding male, below, and a female, above.

Index

About the Author/Illustrator

Todd Telander is a natural-ist illustrator/artist living in Walla Walla, Washington. He has studied and illustrated wildlife since 1988 while liv-ing in California, Colorado, New Mexico, and Washington State. He graduated from the University of California at Santa Cruz with degrees in Biology, Environmental Studies, and Scientific Illustration and has since illustrated numerous books and other publications.

His wife, Kirsten Telander, is a writer and teacher; they have two boys, Miles and Oliver. Todd's work can be viewed online at www .toddtelander.com.